Biblical Sex,

What the Bible Says and Doesn't Say About
Sex and Marriage

OTHER BOOKS BY WALTER LAMP

Biblical Verses, A Frank Study of the Old Testament and Hebrew Bible
- How the Bible and the Religion Changed Over Time
- What the Old Testament / Hebrew Bible Actually Says
- Explaining the Conflicts and Inconsistencies in the Bible
- Better Understanding All the Abrahamic Religions;
  - Judaism, Christianity and Islam

JUDAISM
- How Beliefs Changed From The First Bible Ever Written To Today's Old Testament / Hebrew Bible
- What It Means for Modern Judaism, Christianity and Islam

The TAMAR BIBLE, The First Judeo-Christian Scripture
- The First Bible Ever Written
- Buried In Today's Bible
- Extracted Without Changing or Adding a Single Word and Without Changing The Word Order
- Plus Commentary and Notes on Extraction Methodology

TAMAR, First Author of the Bible
- The Raped Daughter of King David Writes the First Bible
- Invents Feminism
- Reveals the Original Judaism

Koranic Verses, A Frank Study of the Koran
- How the Koran is Honored & Dishonored in Practice
- Understanding Islam's History

99 Prescriptions for a More Ethical Society
- Combating the Major Ethical Abuses of the Day
  - Governance, Excessive Compensation, Subsidies, Lies and Spins, Information Suppression & More

Biblical Sex,

What the Bible Says and Doesn't Say About Sex and Marriage

Discusses Homosexuality and Gay Marriage
Helps You Evaluate Current Issues

By Walter Lamp, J.D. (Yale)

RunningLight Publishing Company
Reno, Nevada.

The Scripture quotations contained herein are from the New Revised Standard Version Bible, copyright © 1989 by the Division of Christian Education of the National Council of Churches of Christ in the U.S.A., and are used by permission. All rights reserved. Other quotations are from the King James Bible of 1611 and are identified as such.

Biblical Sex, What the Bible Says and Doesn't Say About Sex and Marriage by Walter Lamp 1st Edition. Includes bibliographical references and indices.

1. Bible- Old Testament / Hebrew Bible. 2. Judaism – Bible.
3. Christianity – Bible. 4. Biblical Commentary.
5. Sex. 6. Marriage. 7. Homosexuality.

ISBN-13: 978-0-9834954-3-7 (paperback)

Library of Congress Control Number: 2012910569

296 LAM 2012 10 9 8 7 6 5 4 3 2

Printed in the United States of America

Table of Contents

Preface

The clergy are not prudes when it comes to sex. In most religions, clergies offer sexual advice. However, even well-meaning advice is sometimes presented as a religious requirement mandated by Scripture, which might or might not prove to be the case when the Scripture is examined. There is a significant difference between good advice and compulsory requirements.

This book addresses only what one Scripture says about sex and marriage. That Scripture is the Old Testament, which is also known as the Hebrew Bible for they are essentially the same in content and verse numbers. Thus, Jews and Christians have the same background. Christians added the New Testament (the combined Old and New Testaments are referred to as the "Christian Bible" in this book) which provides some sexual material, but most comes from the Old Testament. The focus of this book will be solely the Bible; that is, the Old Testament / Hebrew Bible.

It should be noted that Muslims also refer back to the Old Scriptures although Allah (God in Arabic) has at times abrogated and substituted something like it or better (Koran 2.106). The Koran, the Scripture of Islam, states that Allah also revealed the Torah and the Gospels (Koran 3.3). The four Gospels are the first part of the New Testament. The Torah refers to the first five books of the Hebrew Bible (Genesis, Exodus, Leviticus, Numbers and Deuteronomy[*]), and thus the discussion here would also be of direct interest to Muslims (Koran 5.48, 2.136).

The important thing about going back to the Bible is that, without it, everyone can define his or her religion any way he or she wants. The Bible, the only divine source we have, should define the religion. That is the purpose and use of Scripture. The Bible is the core of the religion and should be observed. Nothing in the Bible provides authority to rewrite that divine writing.

Quotes in this book, *Biblical Sex*, come from the New Oxford Bible (technically the "New Revised Standard Version Bible") written by the National Council of Churches of Christ in the U.S.A. While other translations (or versions) of the Bible are essentially the same, the New Oxford Bible was chosen for use in this book because the author considered it to be the most widely available Bible in the most modern English. In the six translations used in studying the Bible, few meaningful translation differences were encountered; where pertinent, those differences were noted and discussed.

The role of this book is not to give any advice. The sole focus and purpose is to point out what is and is not stated in the Bible itself so that readers might cut though all the gloss that surrounds the Bible. Only the literal meaning of the plain words of the Bible is presented in this book because any interpretation other than the literal is largely a matter of personal belief and faith since each person interprets as she or he chooses.

---

[*] These five books are sometimes called the "Pentateuch" of the Old Testament.

Introduction

We hear a chorus of voices interpreting the Bible one way or another, particularly as to sexual matters. Many of us are at a loss as to what to believe. The choice facing us is either to accept the interpretation being offered or reject it on a gut basis since we have no way to judge what is correct. As a rule, we are not told that we are being offered a personal view or being offered an agenda-based interpretation of the Bible. What we are told is usually well meaning, but not always in accord with the Bible.

THIS BOOK SHUNS ALL INTERPRETATION by relying on the literal meaning of the plain words used in the Bible This book does not take issue with the interpretation of others, but rather provides you, the reader, with the literal meaning of the Bible so that you can evaluate the interpretations otherwise being offered to you, or being forced on you.

You need to understand what the Bible actually does say, because this Scripture is the very core of your religion. The Bible is divine, the only divine writing we have. Only the Bible presents the words inspired by God and, for that reason alone, should be given primary weight. If you care to build on it, you should be free to do so -- but you should know that you would entering onto shaky ground and you shouldn't be too absolute in your views. Others will have their own interpretations. However, all of us should be able to agree on what the plain words of the Bible literally say and don't say, and that alone is the focus of this book.

Words do have meaning, including the words actually found in the Bible. It cannot be assumed that interpreters of the Bible know more or better understand the words God inspired in His Holy Book than God Himself. It cannot be assumed that God was not capable of having His Holy Book written clearly, or that He needed to rely on interpretations to get His message across. If you accept the Bible, you should accept that God had it written so that you could understand the plain meaning of the plain words He had used.

THE BIBLE DOES NOT COVER EVERY ASPECT OF SEXUAL ACTIVITY, and certainly not every nuance. Where the Bible is silent, where the Bible does not address a matter, we are free to fill in the gap as we will -- not as an interpretation, but as a matter of personal belief and faith in full knowledge that others will do likewise. On the same token, where the Bible does address a matter, we cannot ignore it. We must, at least, take it into account before we embellish on it. So the first order of business must be the exploration of what the Bible actually does and doesn't say.

We all see things through our own glasses and our personal beliefs might not be in accord with what the Bible literally says. Knowing what the Bible does say expands understanding and eventually places us on firmer ground. Hiding, burying or ignoring material has never been the way to greater understanding and faith. The proposition advanced in this book is to believe what you want to believe, but at least be aware of what the Bible does say.

WE RUN INTO TRANSLATION COMPLICATIONS because the Bible, in this case the Old Testament and Hebrew Bible on which this book is based, dates back thousands of years. None of the originals are available so experts in translation have to deal with copies of copies of text written in a number of ancient languages. These experts are tremendously knowledgeable as they spend their careers on this. For the most part the experts agree with one another. The words used may and do differ, but the gist will be the same except in rare instances when meaningful translation differences arise. When such translation differences arise, they are noted and discussed in this book. Thus, there is no need to learn the ancient languages and spend the time to duplicate the turf of the translation experts. That would undoubtedly entail a lifetime endeavor and probably be unproductive for the study of language itself would limit the time available to study content.

THE BIBLE WAS WRITTEN over span of some 800 years. As a matter of personal belief and faith, some believers say that the Bible was handed down in its entirety by God to Moses on Mount Sinai, but that would hardly explain the Bible's coverage of King David who came so much later. Although there is no general agreement as to what was handed down on Mount Sinai, it might have only been the Ten Commandments. But that tells only a small part of the story.

The orally transmitted religion was first reduced to writing about 1000 BCE. Generations of priests made additions to that first writing, which is here called the first Bible. It is this multiple authorship of the Bible that accounts for much of the conflicts, inconsistencies, and repetitions found on the very face of the Bible. Fortunately, there isn't too much of this and, for the most part, the plain words of the Bible are clear.

Because the prior writings were considered sacred, the priests could not or would not change or eliminate any words of the first Bible. So they just added their voluminous text to it. They added a word or much more here and there throughout the Bible, not only at the beginning or the end. As a result the original text of the first Bible was not changed but was effectively buried in today's Bible, like the Bible you have in your home.

Perhaps the best illustration of what happened is to be found in the well known story of Abraham being commanded by God to sacrifice (kill) his son Isaac. The sacrifice was aborted by God at the last moment. What isn't frequently noted is that God referred to Isaac as being Abraham's only son, not just once but three times (Genesis 22.2, 22.12, and 22.15). However, Abraham had another son; his firstborn son was Ishmael (Genesis 16.15). Calling Isaac Abraham's only son is an unmistakable "error" right on the face of the Bible that could not have been there through oversight or ignorance over the centuries and not corrected by now.

Fortunately, this "error" has a rational explanation. It was caused by the multiple authorship of the Bible. A later author added the Ishmael text to the Bible and was not able to correct or change the previous writings which were, by then, considered sacred. In this fashion, the original text of the Bible remained intact, buried in today's Bible, including the statements that Isaac was the only son.

It became possible to extract the original text from today's Bible and thus uncover the first Bible. The author had done so[*] and the full text of that first Bible is presented in the Appendix to this book. It was particularly useful in determining how the Bible changed over time and the insights that could be gotten from that, including an enhanced understanding as to how the Bible dealt with sex and marriage.

---

[*] The author's book was called "*THE TAMAR BIBLE, The First Judeo-Christian Scripture,*" because the author believed that Tamar, the raped daughter of King David, was the first author of the Bible. That is, Tamar was the person who first put into writing the theretofore orally transmitted religion. As the identification of Tamar as being the first author and calling her writing the "Tamar Bible" is irrelevant to this book, *Biblical Sex*, the author reverted to calling it the first Bible. The first author of the Bible used the name "Yahweh" for God, so that author is sometimes called the "Yahwist" and the first Bible called the "Yahwist Bible."

The book, *THE TAMAR BIBLE*, delineates the methodology used by the author in extracting the text of the first Bible from today's Bible. The author lifted out words from today's Bible without adding or changing a single word and without changing the order of the words; and the text proved to be fully coherent, perfectly recognizable and smoothly readable as can be seen in the Appendix.

Chapter One

Sex in the Bible*

The ancient society was a promiscuous one, as far as men were concerned. Men could and did have as many wives as they wanted in addition to any number of concubines, and they could also avail themselves of prostitutes. There were male and female prostitutes, even temple or ritual prostitutes. Homosexuality was widespread, but bisexuality would be a better term as the men did have wives and concubines, and there were children.

Married women could only have sex with their one husband. Young women were obligated to remain virgins. However, there were female prostitutes, some being forced into it by their fathers. Although it undoubtedly existed, nothing was said in the Bible about lesbianism. The Bible doesn't address the specifics of female sexuality except to forbid bestiality.

Women were basically the property of men, the husband owning the wife and the father owning the daughter. They were

---

* By way of prologue, the first part of this chapter highlights some of the content discussed in later chapters. The pertinent proofs, quotes and citations, are in the later chapters. The second part of this chapter illustrates the scope of the sexual narratives found in the Bible by providing short synopses of interesting stories.

protected as other chattels were protected. The daughter was obligated to remain a virgin, which maximized the property right the father had in her. The father received a bride-price for giving his daughter in marriage, or, if he wished, he could use her to make an alliance or even cast her into prostitution. The husband's property right in his wife was protected by a presumably effective deterrent; the law subjected the wife to death if she had sexual relations with any other male and also subjected the male to death. A man could have many wives without it being considered adultery.

Marriage, intermarriage and divorce took place freely, evidently as a matter of community tradition and custom since no biblical provisions controlled these matters. There was no biblical law requiring or defining marriage. The priestly additions to the Bible ranted against intermarriage, but there was no law forbidding it. The Bible recognized that divorce existed and never said that marriage couldn't be cast aside; but also never delineated when marriage could be cast aside, although it appeared to have been at the husband's will.

The use of force in sex was recognized, and the biblical penalty was to force marriage. Rape existed, even gang rapes. All kinds of sexual activity must have existed, even bestiality for otherwise it would not have been addressed in the Bible.

THE PRIESTS ADDED THEIR OWN TEXT TO THE FIRST BIBLE, when they came on scene. They aimed at changing some of the traditions and customs of the ancient community and they had varying degrees of success. To understand what happened in biblical terms and how the priests changed the Bible requires explanation.

The Bible is the only document that dates back to that ancient time and place. It is the only source document we have, made as reliable as the human hand could make it over centuries of making copies of copies and translations of translations. It is the only source used in this book.

The Bible was written over a period of more than 800 years. The first writing of the Bible was taken from the oral transmissions of the people, as the people had passed on the religion verbally for centuries from generation to generation. The religion was first recorded in writing during the time of King David, circa 1000 BCE, about two centuries or so after the Phoenicians invented the alphabet. That first writing is here called the first Bible and it covered the period from the Creation to the death of King David.

About two centuries after the first Bible was written, the priests started to make additions to it. They did not merely add to the beginning or end of the first Bible but instead made insertions here and there, anywhere in the Bible. They would add a single word, a phrase, a full sentence, a paragraph or a whole chapter, even complete books like Leviticus and Deuteronomy.

The first Bible was in circulation in the local communities, presumably limited to the elite and educated since each scroll had to be hand written by scribes. Since it was considered a sacred writing, the priests couldn't or wouldn't delete or change a word appearing in the first Bible, but they could and did add to it. The priests' additions were aimed at changing the religion to what they thought best, and those additions were voluminous; in time far greater in size than the first Bible. An illustration of how the priests could change the tenor of the previous writing without dropping or changing a single word in the first Bible is presented in the next chapter.

THE FIRST BIBLE WAS OPEN AND FRANK ABOUT SEX, sometimes bordering on the unseemly, but it didn't go into detail. The focus of the first Bible was on obtaining the land the people were to live in (the Promised Land). It was the priests who added the law (the so-called "laws of Moses") to the Bible in their effort to transform the religion from one revolving around the land to one revolving around the law.* This was done by adding the Mount Sinai and other narratives that inserted into the first Bible the Ten Commandments and other text that contained laws, and through the addition of the Books of Leviticus and Deuteronomy.

The priests also made additions to the first Bible's story narratives. However, few of those additions were specific enough to constitute law. Of course, if the priests wanted to establish or impose something as a matter of law, they could have done so, as they did in the Book of Exodus before the Books of Leviticus and Deuteronomy were added.

So much of what the priests said or implied in their story narrative additions served only to indicate their bent or inclination, as they did not back-up their additions by also adding a definite law as they could have easily done. For instance, the priests never inserted a law forbidding polygamy although they could have done so, but they inserted vague language about "one flesh" in a story narrative that can be viewed as showing their bent against polygamy.

No law barring intermarriage was inserted in the Bible although the priest ranted against it. In the case of homosexuality, the priests did choose to insert a law forbidding it. Perhaps they dared to forbid homosexuality even though it was then widespread in the land, but did not dare to forbid polygamy because it was more deeply and universally ingrained in the male population. Perhaps they did not dare to forbid intermarriage because it would have condemned the marriages of a number of major biblical personalities (like Moses, Judah, and King David).

When the priestly additions were made to the first Bible is unknown. However, much is believed to have been added just before the exile to Babylon and after the return from exile. Both the exile and the return took place in the 6th century BCE, some 4 centuries after the first Bible was written.

---

* The author proves this to be the case in his book "*Biblical Verses, A Frank Study of the Old Testament and Hebrew Bible.*"

The priests made additions to the first Bible that started to allude to sex and brought up fathers, mothers and wives at a point in the Bible when there were only two people on earth, Adam and Eve, and sexual intercourse hadn't yet taken place. The additions looked forced because the biblical story at that point was only about working in the garden and not eating the forbidden fruit. However the priests wanted to mold sex/marriage/family their way and they pursued their purpose as early as they could in the Bible. These priestly additions were vague, only suggestive, and deliberately so because they were not backed up by the addition of definitive laws. Thus, for instance, there is no requirement of marriage in the Bible, no definition as to what marriage was or who could and could not be married.

SOME NARRATIVES OF THE FIRST BIBLE portrayed unseemly sexual events. These narratives likely embarrassed the righteous priests who later reacted to them.

- Abraham[*] fibbed about his wife Sarah being his sister, resulting in the Pharaoh marrying Sarah and adding her to his harem, while enriching Abraham with gifts (Genesis 12.10-20). The priests added a narrative (Genesis 20) to the first Bible that parallels the first Bible story but absolves Abraham from his wife-to-sister fib. In the priestly narrative Sarah wasn't sexually violated, but that cannot cleanse the violation of Sarah in the first Bible narrative. Absolving Abraham was important and that may have been the purpose of the added narrative.

- King David had an adulterous affair with Bathsheba making her pregnant. He then had Bathsheba's husband killed and he married Bathsheba. She had the child, who was Solomon

[*] At that time, Abraham was named "Abram" and Sarah named "Sarai." Their names were changed by God in later priestly additions to the first Bible (Genesis 17.5, 17.15). To avoid confusion, only the names Abraham and Sarah are used in this book.

(2 Samuel 11.1-27). After the priestly additions to the narrative adequately berated King David (2 Samuel 12.1-14) for his nefarious acts, the priests portrayed the child of the adulterous affair as having died and another child conceived who was named Solomon (2 Samuel 12.15-24). The righteous priests couldn't accept that the next king to be crowned would be a child of adultery and apparently felt they had to recast the story.*

As it turned out, the priests first praised King Solomon to the upmost (he was the wisest man on earth), ending with the famous Queen of Sheba narrative (1 Kings 10). Thereafter, King Solomon was severely condemned by the priests in many ways with God finally splitting his kingdom into two parts upon his death. Solomon's mismanagement and extravagance likely led to the weakening of the nation. The Egyptians sacked Jerusalem a mere five years after his death and ultimately the entire Promised Land was lost to the Assyrians and the Babylonians.

In three instances, the women of the first Bible used their cunning and intelligence to determine the future of the entire nation. This was something the righteous priests probably couldn't condone because the women used deception, lies and disobedience or because the women weren't adhering to their subservient role in that male dominated society.

- In the first Bible, Rebekah used lies and deception to steal for her favorite second-born son (Jacob) the birthright that would naturally flow to her first-born son (Esau) who was favored by her husband, the second Patriarch Isaac (Genesis 27). Jacob became the third Patriarch, his twelve sons becoming the twelve tribal leaders of the new nation. The priests

---

* The author of the first Bible had recorded the oral transmissions of the people during the time of King David and stopped writing upon the death of King David (1 Kings 2.46). The priests alone wrote thereafter (1 Kings 3 etc).

sanitized this first Bible narrative by adding that God forecast that the elder son will serve the younger son (Genesis 25.23), making it appear that Rebekah was doing God's bidding. In this fashion the priests righteously absolved Rebekah from her improper acts.

- While the normal succession would have given King David's throne to an older son by another wife, Bathsheba lied to King David so as to get the crown for her son. Bathsheba told David that he had sworn to make her son Solomon the next king (1 Kings 1.15-21), and the very old and feeble King David honored his supposed vow (1 Kings 1.30). Bathsheba was recast by the priestly additions as the pawn of the prophet Nathan, and not the originator of the lie, by merely having her statement appear to repeat what Nathan told her to say (1 Kings 1.13). It could have been the priest's righteousness in converting Bathsheba's lie into the will of a prophet of God. Or perhaps the priests aimed at stilling the voice of a woman who determined the path of the nation, a woman who shouldn't have a voice in that male dominated society, especially an adulteress.

- But perhaps the most important, and certainly the most controversial, was the role Eve played in obtaining knowledge for mankind by her disobedience to God. The first Bible had God compassionately accepting what Eve had done by not killing as He had said He would if the forbidden fruit were eaten (Genesis 2.17) and by God Himself clothing Adam and Eve (Genesis 3.21). This was before God cast them out of the garden so that they couldn't also get at the fruit of the tree of eternal life (Genesis 3.22-24). God gave Adam and Eve freedom to roam the world as they would because God did not then restrain them with any demands or laws or exact any penalties.

That act of Eve, done for her own stated reasons (Genesis 3.6), none of which was suggested by the serpent (Genesis

3.4-5), made Eve the moving party, relegated Adam to merely being a follower, and set the path of humankind. The righteous priests couldn't let the disobedience stand unpunished, particularly as they had adopted a fear-of-God theme (discussed later), so they added punishments (Genesis 3.14-19) to the first Bible's Garden of Eden narrative.

Other first Bible narratives told sexually related stories that did not seem to offend the righteous priests because the priests added no comments or counters to what the first Bible portrayed.

- Amnon rapes his half-sister Tamar and their father, King David, does nothing (2 Samuel 13.21).
- Absalom kills his half-brother, Amnon, who raped his full-sister Tamar (1 Samuel 13.28-29) and goes on to challenge his father for the crown.
- Samson's wife is given by her Philistine father to another man as a wife (Judges 15.2). Samson punishes the Philistines (Judges 15.4-5) and the Philistines punish the father (Judges 15.6). Samson is bested by Delilah in a sexual duel of wits (Judges 16.4-21).
- The men of Gibeah turn out for homosexual gang rape and wind up committing heterosexual gang rape (Judges 19). God does not intervene.

THE PRIESTS ALSO MADE UNSEEMLY ADDITIONS of a sexual nature to the first Bible. In each instance, a possibly thin but righteous justification is found.

- The men of Sodom turn out for homosexual gang rape, which does not take place, and yet God destroys the entire city and everyone in it (Genesis 19). This was a take-off narrative based on the Gibeah narrative where God did not kill (Judges 19). The exact purpose of the priestly Sodom and Gomorrah narrative was not made clear. However, it was made perfectly clear that the priests were endeavoring to chase-down the existence of a grave sin in Sodom, which was found to exist although the sin was never specified.

- Lot's two daughters raped him and bore children sired by him (Genesis 19.30-38). Enemy tribes, presumed evil, descend from the children. Thus, in their righteousness, the priests show that an evil act begets evil fruit, using an unseemly way to get there.

- Tamar tricks her father-in-law Judah into having sexual intercourse with her by disguising and offering herself to him as a prostitute (Genesis 38). In their righteousness, the priests had the right thing done in terms of following the law, even though the narrative extols the cunning and intelligence of a woman. The narrative also shows that the priests were not prudes, or, at least, that generation of priests wasn't.

- Jonathan's love for King David was wonderful and better than the love of a woman according to King David, and King David greatly loved him (2 Samuel 1.26). Nowhere did the priests comment on or try to counter this and other indications of the homosexual relationship between King David and Jonathan although a priest of a later generation condemned homosexuality (Leviticus 18.22, 30.13).

Some of the priestly additions to the first Bible related to sexual events appear to condone the excessive or unseemly.

- A number of local men take up with foreign women and God casts a plague against the entire community, indiscriminately killing 24,000 of His own people (Numbers 25.1-9).

- The men of Benjamin forcibly abduct hundreds of virgins as planned and sanctioned by the community (Judges 21.16-21).

- Jacob's daughter, Dinah, is raped by a prince who offers to marry her and pay a high bride-price (Genesis 34.12). The prince appears to want to do the proper thing, which is just what the law in Exodus 22.16 and Deuteronomy 22.28 would later require. But Jacob's sons kill the prince and all the males of his city (Genesis 34.25-26).

The foregoing summaries serve to indicate the wide scope of sexual activity portrayed in the Bible. Sex does seem to play a large role in biblical narratives.

Chapter Two

Putting-Down Women

Put-downs of women come in the form of social discrimination, unequal treatment under law, ignoring a woman's voice or existence, subjugating females to males, and in a variety of other practices. The Bible clearly puts-down the female gender with most people believing that, in this, the Bible merely reflected the ancient male-dominated society.

However, it is up to historians, archeologists and other scientists to tell us whether the Bible reflected the then existing society. If the scientific evidence is insufficient, it might have been that the Bible contributed to molding the ancient society (rather than the society contributing to the molding of the Bible). In the very early stages of the religion, when the first Bible was written in about 1000 BCE, it is likely that both possibilities existed as the societal scientific evidence is scant. While good societal scientific evidence about latter times abounds, it cannot be assumed that society was always that way.

While this would be an interesting exploration, it would be beyond the scope of this book, *Biblical Sex*. This book does not explore what might have been happening in the secular world, but rather focuses only on what the Bible says or does not say about the secular world and accepts that as being the case.

How the priests' additions to the Bible changed the tenor of the Bible is described for the purpose of showing how the societal aspects of the religion developed in the Bible itself, not to show what actually happened in the ancient society. Again, the focus here is only on the Bible and what it says, and only that.

In the First Bible

In the first Bible, God is referred to in male terms. It is always He or Him. It might just be the literary style of the first author, but that is just speculation and the fact remains that God is referred to in male terms.

MALES WERE IN THE FOREFRONT of biblical narrative. God first created the male. Creation of the woman almost appears to have been an afterthought.

> **"… [T]he LORD God formed man from the dust of the ground, and breathed into his nostrils the breath of life; and the man became a living being. And the LORD GOD planted a garden in Eden, in the east; and there he put the man whom he had formed." (Genesis 2.7-8)**

> **"The LORD God took the man and put him in the garden of Eden to till it and kept it. (Genesis 2.15)**

> **"Then the LORD God said,** 'It is not good that the man should be alone; **I will make him a helper** as his partner.' **So out of the ground the LORD God**

formed every animal of the field and every bird of the air, and brought them to the man to see what he would call them; and whatever the man called every living creature, that was its name. The man gave names to all cattle, and to the birds of the air, and to every animal of the field; **but for the man there was not found a helper** as his partner. **So the LORD God caused a deep sleep to fall on the man, and he slept; then he took one of his ribs, and closed up its place** with flesh. **And the rib that the LORD God had taken from the man he made into a woman** and brought her to the man." **(Genesis 2.18-22)**

Readers should notice that part of the forgoing quote is in bold type and part is in ordinary type. It is important to now take the time to explain what this is all about because it permeates the entire Bible.

The foregoing quote is from today's Bible and thus contains both first Bible text and text added by the priests. The bold type highlights the text that dates back to the first Bible and the ordinary type was used for the text added by the priests.

This presentation illustrates what happened in the writing of the Bible and shows how the priests went about changing the Bible. This is the only time in this book where both bold and ordinary type is used in quotes.

In all other quotations in this book, only the bold type will be used and, unless otherwise noted, the text would be from today's Bible, like the Bible you would have at home today.

As will later become pertinent, readers can see from this presentation that in the first Bible there was no mention of the woman being a partner, there was no talk about birds or naming the animals (which does seem to be superfluous to the story being then told), no talk of flesh, and no talk of bringing the woman to the man.

All these priestly additions were aimed at introducing concepts important to the priests and doing it in a fashion that would not require changing any word of the first Bible.

Women were made differently, and of different material. Whether the making of the woman was an afterthought or not, it is clear that the woman was made from the man's rib, not made of the same stuff (the dust of the earth) as the man was made of. This could lead to the thought that the woman was somehow the less. That would be pure speculation as the first Bible made no such statement.

It could be said that the woman was indirectly made of the same stuff as man or, if the cloning analogy is used,* the clone was equal in all respects to the original because the genders are equal. As the first Bible is silent on the matter, everyone is free to believe or make-up what they want.

Nevertheless, the thought persists that the woman is somewhat the less because of the way she was created. The next narrative, the Garden of Eden narrative, contradicts this by speaking of at least basic gender equality. The woman, Eve, took the lead in that narrative and the man, Adam, appeared to be of no account (Genesis 3.1-7), demonstrating that the woman was not inferior and possibly superior.

---

* Cloning becomes a very interesting conjecture in a tangential respect. Cloning duplicates, so the woman couldn't be a clone because there was a gender change. Unless, that is, the man had androgynous characteristics of both genders. Ancient mythologies had such beings. Thus, cloning based on the androgynous characteristics of the first man could underlay the cloning analogy.

What makes such a proposition particularly interesting is that man was formed in the likeness of God, as the priests would later indicate in their addition (Genesis 1.26) to the first Bible. If the cloning analogy is used with the first man having androgynous characteristics, so too could God also be said to have androgynous characteristics. That would tangentially support the argument that God was both male and female, which some believers do believe. That would eliminate the put-down that God was referred to in the Bible in male terms, making that a matter of literary style or convenience.

Yet, men remained in the forefront and God spoke to the males. God spoke to females only when they had to enter the narrative. For instance, God continually spoke to Adam (Genesis 2.16, 3.9, 3.11) and spoke to Eve only after Adam said that she gave him the forbidden fruit to eat (Genesis 3.12-13). God did not even bother to send Eve from the garden, explicitly speaking about and expelling only Adam (Genesis 3.22-24). Perhaps this omission was due to the conciseness of the first Bible, because it later became obvious that Eve also left the garden. Nevertheless, it is clear that the male had the biblical focus.

THE MALE WAS GENERALLY THE MOVING PARTY in the first Bible, like in Abraham taking his wife along with him (Genesis 12.5) when he left his father's house (Genesis 12.1). Thus there was a male orientation from the very beginning.

Yet, Eve was the moving party in the Garden of Eden narrative, with Adam essentially doing what Eve indicated (Genesis 3.6). This later proved to be the first contradiction to the proposition that only a male could be the party who determined the path of nations.

The male initiated sexual activity as shown in the case of Adam knowing his wife (Genesis 4.1), the men taking wives for themselves (Genesis 6.2), Isaac taking his wife (Genesis 24.67), and so forth. The male chose the wife (i.e., Jacob choosing his wife in Genesis 29.18) although his father, another male, might choose the bride for him. For example, Abraham chose Isaac's wife (Genesis 24.4). From the beginning, it was never the wife choosing the husband or, for that matter, having any say in the choice.

GIFTS WERE GIVEN BY THE MALE when he took a wife (Genesis 12.15-16, 24.10) or he rendered services in lieu of a gift if he had nothing to give (Genesis 29.18, 29.30, Exodus 2.21). Those gifts/services to the father might be viewed as payment for the daughter, evolving into what the priests later called the bride-price (e.g., Exodus 22.16).

The priests used a much more monetarily oriented approach as seen by their requiring a payment of 50 shekels in silver (Deuteronomy 22.28) to the father when the daughter is given in marriage. They even used a duel pricing-system with a different "bride-price for virgins" (Exodus 22.16-17) under special circumstances involving the seduction of the daughter.

In the first Bible, what appeared to be a true "gift" and not a payment in exchange for the woman appeared in one instance. The Pharaoh voluntarily gave gifts to Sarah's "brother" Abraham after Sarah had already been taken into the Pharaoh's harem (Genesis 12.15-16). It was also shown to be a gift by the Pharaoh not demanding its return when the Pharaoh discovered that Sarah was Abraham's wife and not his sister. The Pharaoh returned Sarah to Abraham and kicked them out of Egypt, Abraham then being rich (Genesis 12.19-13.2).

AS THE HEAD OF HOUSEHOLD, the male made the decisions for the family. Abraham alone decided to leave his father's house and take his wife Sarah with him (Genesis 12.5). Although he was tricked, Isaac alone made the decision as to which son would have the blessing that determined family inheritance (Genesis 27.37). Jacob alone decided when and where his household would go (e.g., Genesis 45.28-46.1).

There wasn't much more in the first Bible that addressed the male-female relationship or how the people lived. God hadn't issued any commands directing the people after His first and only command not to eat the forbidden fruit (Genesis 2.17) was disobeyed. God's commandments, laws and ordinances making demands on the people and restricting how the people lived were added by the priests to the first Bible much later.

In The Priests' Additions to the First Bible

The priests added much to the first Bible showing that the ancient society then put-down women or by revealing that the priests and God[*] would have it so.

BRINGING THE WOMAN TO THE MAN is a clear biblical put-down of women, an early priestly addition to the first Bible's Creation narrative. It wasn't enough to just create the woman as a helper to the man, as the first Bible had it, or even as a partner of the man which the priests added, but the priests obviously felt that they had to start inserting their gender, sex and marriage views into the biblical narrative.

> **"And the rib that the LORD God had taken from the man he made into a woman <u>and brought her to the man</u>." [Emphasis added.] (Genesis 2.22)**

There was no need to add that the woman was brought to the man. It was an allusion to sex, and it seems to be a rather gratuitous statement. It was superfluous and unnecessary to the story then being told. There were just two people on earth at that time and the focus was on working in the Garden of Eden, not on sex and reproduction.

While the implication behind bringing the woman to the man was sexual, it did not imply an equal relationship, a loving relationship or togetherness. It implied subjugation of the woman to

---

[*] The Bible is considered divine only because God inspired the various authors who recorded God's inspired thoughts in writing. That inspiration is what makes the Bible God's Holy Book, with God being the true author.

For convenience in writing this book, *Biblical Sex*, no reference is made to God's inspiration being behind every priestly addition mentioned. But it must be understood that God did inspire each addition to His Bible.

the man, which was soon confirmed by another priestly put-down of women.

WIVES WERE TO BE RULED BY THEIR HUSBANDS

(Genesis 3.16) according to the penalties the priests added to the first Bible's Garden of Eden narrative.

The first Bible had portrayed God as being compassionate because He did not kill Adam and Eve for eating the forbidden fruit, as He had said* He would (Genesis 2.17), and also because He made garments for them and clothed them (Genesis 3.21). This was before God sent them off from the garden (Genesis 3.24) into the open world, also compassionately free of constraints. All this compassion flew in the face of the priests' desire to portray a fearsome God so as to instill the fear of God in the people for another purpose.† Thus, it is believed that the penalties were added to the Garden of Eden narrative so as to counter God's compassion portrayed in the first Bible. A very compassionate God would not be very fearsome.

Nonetheless, the biblical punishments the priests inserted into the narrative subjected men to endlessly toil in the ground, which essentially continued the role Adam had in the garden, albeit with perhaps more difficulty and discomfort (Genesis 3.17-19). Women were to encounter increased pain in childbearing. As a second and independent punishment, a wife would be ruled by her husband (Genesis 3.16). This subjugated the wife to her husband. This was an extra punishment for the woman and it stands out.

Although women were being put-down at the earliest opportunity the priests had to do so, at the time of the Garden of Eden narrative, the first Bible did not then portray the woman as

---

* God mostly spoke to and about the man, Adam, although the context may have also involved the woman.

† For instance, "all that violence" was inserted into the first Bible so that the people would fear God and better comply with all the laws the priests added to the first Bible. This is explained in detail in the author's book "*Biblical Verses, A Frank Study of the Old Testament and Hebrew Bible.*"

being inferior to the man. But for the added punishments, the priests largely left the first Bible Garden of Eden narrative alone.

The first Bible portrayed Eve as a heroine for braving the wrath of God in order to provide wisdom and knowledge to humankind. She knowingly took the risk that God would kill as He said He would if the forbidden fruit were eaten (Genesis 2.17). She heroically took the risk that the serpent was wrong in its belief that God would not kill (Genesis 3.4). Eve gave her very own reasons for eating the fruit, none of which was suggested by the serpent (Genesis 3.6). By so doing, Eve delivered to humans the knowledge and wisdom denied them by God.

Adam later confirmed to God that he ate the fruit because Eve gave it to him (Genesis 3.12). Thus, it was Eve who acted and gave reasons for her actions, accomplishing her purpose and portraying a picture of proficiency while Adam did and said nothing and only followed Eve's lead. Eve comes out looking much better than Adam and certainly not inferior to him and not ruled by him.

The priests apparently would not let this stand as their purpose did seem to be putting-down women, and that would have included putting-down Eve. The priests inserted into what Eve said to the serpent that God would kill them if they touched the tree (Genesis 3.3), which God never said (see Genesis 2.16-17) and thus the priests made Eve look foolish.

However, God had only spoken to Adam, and Adam necessarily told Eve about it. So it could well have been Adam who told Eve about not touching the tree, although readers are likely to blame Eve for the error rather than Adam. No reason other than making Eve look foolish could be found or conceived of for the priests adding the superfluous material about touching the tree.

The priests had previously used the word "rule" in their Creation narrative. "Rule" means govern, as in the sun and moon ruling the day and night (Genesis 1.16-18), or it could also mean "dominate" as in humans having domination over every living thing (Genesis 1.28).

Whether men did rule and dominate women in the ancient society, or whether the priests made it so with their additions to the first Bible, is irrelevant. By making this addition to the Bible, which is eternal and cast in stone as is all biblical text, men ruling women became a religious precept that would never change. Partnership and sharing between men and women were effectively excluded.

WOMEN WERE LARGELY IGNORED IN THE BIBLE. The genealogies added by the priests to the Bible (e.g., Genesis 4.17-22, 5.1-32, 10.1-32, 11.10-32 in the Book of Genesis alone) omit the mention of wives and generally ignore the birth of daughters. The genealogies might mention the names of daughters and wives when the women play a particular part in a narrative. All sons were mentioned by name irrespective of whether they had a role to play.

Censuses seemed to be taken for purposes of taxation or war (Numbers 1.2, 2 Samuel 24.2). Women weren't counted, except one census counted a few women who had inherited property because there were no sons (Numbers 26.33). So even for war or taxation, women seemed to be largely disregarded.

Sometimes it was almost as if "the people" excluded women, as shown by Moses addressing "the people" when he came down from Mount Sinai to prepare the people to receive the Ten Commandments from God. He told the people to prepare by not going near a woman (Exodus 19.15), an obvious reference to purification by sexual abstinence, but also showing that Moses was addressing only men when he spoke to "the people."

The "wife" got specific mention in the Ten Commandments prohibition on coveting a neighbor's property. However, the wife was mentioned only as being an item of property includable in the neighbor's household.

"You shall not covet your neighbor's house; you shall not covet your neighbor's wife, or male or female slave, or ox,

or donkey, or anything that belongs to your neighbor."
(Exodus 20.17)

The Ten Commandments' Sabbath requirement, addressed to the adult male as are all of the commandments, forbids everyone in the household from working. This commandment lists the members of the household, specifically including daughters as well as sons, but does not mention wives. It's as if wives didn't exist.

"But the seventh day is a sabbath to the LORD your God; you shall not do any work – you, your son or your daughter, your male or female slave, your livestock, or the alien resident in your towns." (Exodus 20.10)

THE FEMALE VIEW WAS RARELY TAKEN INTO ACCOUNT, or sought. Even when it's just the woman's life and future at stake, her views or opinions were not sought. Only in the Garden of Eden narrative was a man shown to be of no account, doing and saying nothing and not being asked his opinion or desire - - Adam appeared as the non-entity, not Eve. Otherwise, it was the woman who was of no account and ignored.

Dinah was the daughter of the Patriarch Jacob and Leah. Dinah left Jacob's camp to visit the women of Shechem, a city Jacob's clan was passing through, when the local prince seized her by force and lay with her (Genesis 34.1-2). The prince fell in love with her and wanted to marry her (Genesis 34.3-4). He was willing to pay as high a bride-price as Jacob would name (Genesis 34.11-12).

What the Prince of Shechem offered, marriage and a high-bride-price, happened to be just what biblical law would later mandate under such circumstances, with neither the man who violated the daughter nor her father being given any option in the Bible to do otherwise (Deuteronomy 22.28-29). Dinah's brothers were angry about the outrage to their sister and developed a ploy that allowed them to kill the prince and all the other men of Shechem (Genesis 34.25-26), and the city was then plundered (Genesis 34.27).

As a violated woman, Dinah would likely become un-marriageable and lead a desolate life, whereas, as the wife of a prince who loved her, she would likely have a much better life if not a good life. But nobody had asked Dinah what she had wanted done. Her views and desires were of no account.

Where an un-engaged virgin is seduced (as contrasted to the use of force, or rape), marriage and the payment of a bride-price to the father are also required (Exodus 22.16). However, the father is given the option to refuse giving his daughter in marriage and, instead of receiving a bride-price, he would receive a "bride-price for virgins" (Exodus 22.17). It cannot be determined from the Bible itself whether a bride-price paid for the woman in marriage is higher or lower than the "bride-price for virgins" paid as compensation for damage to the father's property right in his daughter's virginity.

That is not important. What is important is that the daughter was not given the option to refuse marriage. Only the father was given the option as to whether his daughter would marry. This serves to corroborate that the Bible gives daughters no say as to their future and it also serves to confirm that the father owns the daughter.

WOMEN ARE TREATED LIKE CHATTELS IN THE BIBLE. The husband owns the wife and the father owns the daughter. The relationships are literally treated in terms of property rights.

As previously noted, the father's property right in the daughter is shown by the requirement that the father be given a bride-price when he gives the daughter in marriage or a "bride-price for virgins" when the daughter is seduced and the father exercises his option not to give the daughter in marriage (Exodus 22.17). The daughter's virginity is effectively treated as being wrapped up in the property right the father has in the daughter, and taking her virginity diminishes his property.

As the daughter is property, the father can sell her as a slave (Exodus 21.7). There is no comparable provision indicating that a son can be sold as a slave.

The father can cast his daughter into prostitution. The father would be profaning her and the land by doing so (Leviticus 19.29), but no penalty can be found in the Book of Leviticus or elsewhere in the Bible for the father making his daughter a prostitute or for her becoming a prostitute. However, should the daughter of a priest become a prostitute, she is subject to a death penalty (Leviticus 21.9). While the Bible makes reference to male prostitutes (see the chapter *"Homosexuality in the Bible"*), there is nothing in the Bible that shows that a father can cast a son into prostitution.

Samson married but his father-in-law continued to maintain authority over Samson's wife, perhaps because she remained with her father when Samson returned to his parent's home. The father-in-law, a Philistine, gave her in marriage to another man (Judges 15.2), defeating Samson's property right in her. Samson could not let this stand (Judges 15.3-5), but neither could the Philistines who killed the father and the daughter (Judges 15.6). A man's property right in a woman had to be protected, and after the daughter married, it was the husband's property right that mattered as the father had already received the bride-price payment for his property right in the daughter.

In only one instance in the Bible was the good of society more important than the preservation of the fathers' property rights in their unmarried daughters. After a war between the tribes, only 600 men of the tribe of Benjamin remained alive while all the women of that tribe were killed. The victors had taken an oath not to give their daughters to Benjaminites and they became concerned that a tribe of their nation would be blotted out in time (Judges 21.3, 21.17) because the remaining Benjaminites would have no wives.

So the victors went to a town that did not fight in the war and killed everyone there except for the 400 virgins who lived in that town. They gave the 400 virgins to the 600 Benjaminites (Judges

21.12) and then devised a plan for the Benjaminites to abduct 200 virgins elsewhere, which plan was executed (Judges 21.23). The victors planned to justify the abduction by asking (telling!) the 200 fathers to be generous (Judges 21.22) and accept the loss of their daughters, which was what happened. The existence of the fathers' property right in their daughters was recognized, but blatantly overridden by those who had the power to do so.

The husband owned the wife. This is even shown in the Ten Commandments which forbids coveting your neighbor's house or wife, or anything else that belongs to your neighbor (Exodus 20.17). The neighbor's wife is treated a possession, just like the slaves and the animals owned by the neighbor are treated.

That people, wives and daughters, can be treated as property is collaborated by the existence of slavery and the laws concerning of slavery. Property rights underlie slavery arrangements. For instance, if an indentured male slave comes single, he leaves single; if he comes married, he leaves with his wife; and if he were given a wife who bore him children, he leaves alone as the master owns the wife and children (Exodus 21.2-4).

PROPERTY RIGHTS REQUIRED PROTECTION, with the father protecting the daughter and the law protecting the wife.

Daughters represented valuable property as they can be worked, "sold" in marriage or used to make worthwhile marriage alliances. As a result, the father has an incentive to protect his investment in his daughter until she is gone from his household. This is shown in the Tamar Rape narrative, where Amnon could not get at his half-sister as she was adequately protected by her father King David (2 Samuel 13.2). So Amnon had to trick King David into bypassing the protective system the king had set up for his daughter (2 Samuel 13.7). Although this was royalty, the daughter would be protected on any social or economic level according to the resources of the father.

The husband's property right in his wife was effectively protected by laws that deterred her violation, whether she was a voluntary participant in the affair or not. A man found lying with another man's wife was to be put to death (Deuteronomy 22.22), whether the man was married or single. If the man were married, it would be called adultery, which also entailed death (Leviticus 20.10). These laws also served as deterrents for the wife, as she too would be put to death if she had sex with any man other than her husband (Deuteronomy 22.22, Leviticus 20.10).

Thus, the wife had an incentive to make herself unavailable to other men and the other men had an incentive to avoid married women. To be sure, the husband lost his property (the wife) if the law were violated, but the law undoubtedly acted as an effective deterrent and thus protected the husband property right in his wife or wives.

The "redemption" laws that provided financial support the priests and their activities were viewed as being grounded in property rights or ownership, this time the ownership right of God. God owned the firstborn sons (Exodus 13.12, 22.29, 34.19-20) who had to be redeemed from Him by their fathers. Only the firstborn sons get such attention, not daughters, which can be viewed as another put-down of women.

In addition to receiving the bride-price payment, the father is also relieved of his obligation to support the daughter when she marries and joins her husband's household.* But this is not necessarily an added benefit as it cannot be forgotten that daughters did chores while in the father's household, like Rebekah drawing water for the household (Genesis 24.15-16) and Rachel keeping her father's sheep (Genesis 29.9).

---

* Although this is beyond the scope of this book, *Biblical Sex*, in later times the father would receive nothing and have to provide a dowry when the daughter married. The dowry could be viewed either as a gift or as a payment made by the father that rids himself of his obligation to support the daughter.

THE INHERITANCE LAWS also favored men. Sons inherit the father's property. Where there is more than one son, the firstborn son is entitled to a double portion even if born of a less-favored wife (Deuteronomy 21.15-17). The father owns it all, with the mother owning nothing or just temporarily holding property for the son(s). Wives inherent nothing from their husbands; it all goes to the sons. Daughters inherit the father's property only where there are no sons (Numbers 27.8). If there are no sons and no daughters, the deceased's brothers inherit; and if there are no brothers, the inheritance goes to the deceased father's brothers and failing that to the nearest kinsman (Numbers 27.9-11).

The property of a woman goes to her husband upon marriage (Numbers 36.3) so the wife winds up losing anything she might have owned or inherited. Thus, a daughter who inherited her father's land (because there were no sons) would see that land go into the hands of another tribe if she married someone of another tribe. That was barred by requiring a daughter who inherited her father's property to marry within her father's tribe (Numbers 36.6-8). Thus, still more discriminatory rules were piled on women.

There is another legal restriction on who a woman might marry. The wife of a husband who died without having a son cannot marry outside the family where the husband's brother is at hand to give her a child (Deuteronomy 25.5). The brother is obligated to give her a son and marry her. It's called "levirate-marriage." The expressly stated biblical purpose behind this required marriage practice is that a son be born bearing the name of the deceased husband (Deuteronomy 25.6) so as to preserve the deceased's name and property. It was not because the wife had any right or entitlement to a child or because she would be comforted by one.

STILL OTHER DISCRIMATIONS AGAINST WOMEN appear in the bible, the scope being very wide.

The purity and other laws added to the first Bible present the clearest gender discrimination, yet those laws could have been well meaning. They likely represented the health beliefs at the time, although not necessarily sound on a scientific basis. But that cannot be said of the purity law that considers a woman bearing a female child to be unclean for twice as long as a woman bearing a male child.

"... If a woman conceives and bears a male child, she shall be ceremonially unclean seven days .... If she bears a female child, she shall be unclean two weeks ...." (Leviticus 12.2-5)

This might or might not be considered punishment for giving birth to a female instead of male child. Otherwise, no rationale comes to mind for such a rule. It is clearly a gender put-down.

Another gender put-down is that the valuation of a male is up to double the valuation of a female for purposes of making a dedication to the temple, (Leviticus 27.1-7).

The treatment of vows presents still another put-down of women. The father may nullify the vows made by his daughter (Numbers 30.3-5). The husband may nullify the vows of his wife, whether made before (Numbers 30.6-8) or after their marriage (Numbers 30.10-15). Widows and divorced women are bound by their vows (Numbers 30.9) showing that they are treated independent entities because nobody owns them, while a wife and a daughter are owned and so have no voice. A man's vow remains standing under all circumstances.

The three women who might be considered matriarchs of the religion, Sarah, Rebekah, and Rachel, were barren (Genesis 11.30, 25.21, 30.22). Other women were also shown to be barren in the Bible, but never was there any mention of a man being incapable of giving a child.

As previously shown, the husband may have many wives, but the wife may have only one husband. The husband can question wife's fidelity by putting her through an ordeal (Numbers 5.11-31) but the wife cannot question the husband. The husband can divorce the wife (Deuteronomy 24.1), but nothing was said about a wife divorcing her husband.

Only female sorcerers were to be killed according to Exodus 18.18, but Leviticus in all its righteousness later created equality by requiring both male and female mediums and wizards be put to death (Leviticus 20.27).

SANITIZING THE "UNSEEMLY" NARRATIVES of the first Bible frequently resulted in the priests putting-down women. The first Bible pulled no punches, showed people with all their warts, and frequently elevated the status of women by giving them major roles that literally determined the future of the people, the nation and the religion.

While the priests put-down women, it cannot be determined whether they were anti-women or only wanted to put things in what to them was their proper place. As the first Bible would present even the leading personalities of the religion in ways that that the priests likely thought to be unseemly, the priests could merely have been sanitizing the offending narratives.

As the wife of a Patriarch, the priests may have felt that Rebekah should have been blameless. But Rebekah's unseemly actions showed her to be otherwise (Genesis 27.5-17). That could have accounted for the priests making an addition to the first Bible (Genesis 25.23) that indicated Rebekah had done what God wanted. The addition served to absolve and restore Rebekah to a proper position. If God had wanted it the way the priests added, there would have been no need for the unseemly tale; God could have had Jacob born first. But the priests were stuck with the unseemly tale that was included in the first Bible. God saying that Esau would serve Jacob, as would be the case if Jacob been born first, was the priestly addition aimed at sanitizing the tale and absolving Rebekah for her bad or evil behavior.

On the other hand, the priests could have had such a low opinion of women that their aim was to negate the proposition that a woman, Rebekah, determined the fate of the religion and the nation by selecting the next Patriarch. After all, it was Rebekah who made her son Jacob the third Patriarch of the religion. Thus, the priest's addition effectively stated that it was God who really determined who the next Patriarch would be, not Rebekah.

A low opinion of woman could also have been the reason for the priests making Eve look foolish with the matter of touching the tree, which supposedly was all the priests could do with the narrative. They could not change what had already been written about Eve in the first Bible as it was considered sacred. Eve had determined the path of the people and all of humanity in a very fundamental way by giving them access to knowledge and wisdom.

It is not clear whether the priests wrote the Tamar/Judah narrative (Genesis 38) because it portrayed how a woman, Tamar, made her mark and actually bested a man. The man was no less than Judah, who gave his name to the largest tribe in the land and to the Kingdom of Judah when the nation was split into two kingdoms after the death of King Solomon (the other was the Kingdom of Israel). Tamar planned and executed her plan perfectly, proving to be the equal of any man in terms of bravery as well as cunning.

This is not the stuff priests normally wrote. But the references to God killing Tamar's husband Er and later killing Er's brother Onan who refused to give Tamar a son by spilling his seed on the ground (giving rise to the term "onanism") would not have appeared in the first Bible. The God portrayed in the first Bible did not kill.

Tamar was entitled to a son under the levirate-marriage practice. Judah, the father of both Er and Onan, kept his third son Shelah from Tamar because his two other sons were taken by God and Judah feared it would also happen to Shelah. Tamar, disguised as a prostitute, attracted the widower Judah and had him give her a son. Initially Judah called for her death for whoredom,[*] which he apparently had a right to do (Genesis 38.24). Judah relented when Tamar proved that Judah was the father, and Judah conceded that he was in the wrong for not giving his third son to Tamar (Genesis 38.25-26). Tamar gave birth to Perez (Genesis 38.29), the ancestor of King David (Ruth 4.18-22).[†]

Thus, Tamar had a material impact on the future of the nation and had bested a man, things the priests would not normally let stand. Perhaps most of the biblical text of the Tamar/Judah narrative did come from the first Bible and the priests just found a way to insert the hand of God in killing Er and Onan without making it appear that they changed sacred text.

The Bathsheba/King David narrative (2 Samuel 11) of the first Bible needed sanitization because it was a blot on the character of King David, who could be accused of adultery and murder. The priestly sanitization took place in two sets of additions. First, much text was added berating King David (2 Samuel 12.7-13) for what he had done. Second, the priests added that God caused the death of the child of the adultery (2 Samuel 12.14-19) as it wouldn't do for that child to later become king. Another son was said by the priests to have been born to King David and Bathsheba and it was this son who was named Solomon (2 Samuel 12.24).

Later, when Solomon was an adult, Bathsheba lied to the aging and feeble King David (1 Kings 1.7) and in doing so tricked King David into making her son king (1 Kings 1.30) although Solomon was not in line for the crown. The priests proved to be

---

[*] The Bible never delineates what the crime of "whoredom" entails or the circumstances that would underlie it. Nevertheless, as no comparable treatment is found in the Bible for men who are promiscuous, it could indicate the existence of still another type of discrimination against women.

[†] And also the ancestor of Joseph, husband to Mary who gave birth to Jesus (Matthew 1.3-6, 1.16).

ambivalent about Solomon, at first extolling him (1 Kings 3 – 10) and then condemning him (1 Kings 11) and splitting his kingdom on his death (1 Kings 11.11-13). Thus, Bathsheba determined the course of the nation, perhaps with negative impact as King Solomon could be blamed for the ultimate fall of the nation to the Assyrians and Babylonians.

What could go unnoticed in the Bathsheba/King David narrative is that Bathsheba might have deliberately attracted King David. King David was walking about on the roof of his palace (2 Samuel 11.2) when he spied Bathsheba bathing in the open. On the same token, those living around the palace could see King David walking on the roof of his palace. The eyes around the place are more likely to focus on the palace than the eyes of the king focus on any spot because there was much more for the king to look at. Bathsheba's bathing must have been very close to the palace for King David to see that she was beautiful (2 Samuel 11.2), and she would have surely seen him. So there is a possibility that Bathsheba deliberately bathed in King David's view, and thus planned what happened. That she was cunning enough to have done this is later confirmed by how she tricked King David into making her son his successor.

Thus the priests both sanitized the narrative by berating King David as they did in the name of God and having God kill the child of the adultery. In their righteousness, the priests would not let a child of adultery become the third king of the nation. And they also wouldn't let a women determine the fate of the nation, so they made it seem that the prophet of God, Nathan, hatched the plot to get the crown for Solomon (1 Kings 11.11-14).

The priests also aimed at sanitizing Abraham's wife-to-sister lie (Genesis 10.13) by adding text to the first Bible claiming that Sarah was in fact Abraham's sister, his half-sister (Genesis 20.12). The priests may have also aimed at restoring Sarah's besmirched reputation by showing that Sarah was not violated (Genesis 20.6).

The priest's narrative (Genesis 20) was too similar to the first Bible narrative (Genesis 10) to be mere coincidence. But what happen between Sarah and Abimelech in the priest's narrative obviously could not bear on what happened between Sarah and Pharaoh in the first Bible narrative.

So the underlying purpose of the narrative the priests added to the first Bible must have been to show that Abraham spoke the truth when he said Sarah was his sister, his half-sister. However, there is nothing in the Bible to support Sarah being a half-sister, and a genealogy written by priests (Genesis 11.27-31) contradicts it. As a result it appears that the priests may have been less than accurate in their effort to erase Abraham's fib.

From a priest's viewpoint, it is likely that only the truth would be expected in the words of the first Patriarch, Abraham, and thus their effort to portray Sarah as being a half-sister. The priests obviously felt that they had to restore Abraham's good reputation, while the first Bible had not concerned itself with such things.

Nonetheless, uncovering rationales behind the written word is always speculative and leads to nothing concrete. So all this speculation about the story narratives of the Bible should be put aside. The plain words of the Bible tell us more than enough about how women were put-down.

Chapter Three

Marriage, Intermarriage and Divorce

The priests attempted to elevate the institution of marriage to a lofty level in the Bible, much higher than it apparently played in the ancient secular society. As the Bible shows, concubines existed alongside wives. Men could and did have more than one wife and also could and did have any number of concubines. Prostitution appeared widespread, and there was even temple or ritual prostitution. The faithful intermarried outside the faith. Husbands could easily divorce wives. Thus, the secular society would make any rhetoric about the institution of marriage appear to be mere rhetoric.

This secular society must have displeased the interventionist priests who made additions to the first Bible so to change the religion in an attempt to mold secular society as they deemed best for the people. The first Bible addressed nothing about how the people should lead their lives, with God providing no directives, commandments or laws while the old religion essentially focused on getting the people a home, the Promised Land. The first Bible did use husband/wife terminology, showing that the concept of marriage did exist, but that was about it.

Other than the Bible itself, not many writings date back to that time and place so there is no way to determine how aggressively the priests actually were in attempting to remold the secular society. We don't have much hard information on that secular society. Most of what we know about the secular society comes from the Bible itself, namely the additions made by priests of many generations and thus written at different times.

The priests couldn't have been too aggressive, or they feared going further than they went in their additions, because they never added any commandment, law, or other directive requiring marriage, defining marriage, or specifying who could and couldn't get married.

The priestly additions were vague at best. The priests added the concept of "one flesh" and clinging to one's wife to the first Bible some time after it was written in the age of King David, about 1000 BCE. At that time, men having many wives and concubines appeared to be the order of the day. King David had six wives who gave him sons while he was at Hebron (2 Samuel 3.2-5) and had one previous wife who gave him no sons (1 Samuel 18.27). He took an unspecified number of additional wives (which would have included Bathsheba) and concubines after he moved to Jerusalem (2 Samuel 5.13), the concubines numbering at least ten (2 Samuel 15.16).

This biblical text described the secular society, making it difficult for the priests to insist on monogamous marriage or any other constraints. So the priests used the vague "one flesh" language, adding no laws requiring or governing marriage or making marriage ordained by God. God did not require marriage.

Similarly, the priests inserted much into the first Bible condemning intermarriage, but with intermarriage being part of the fabric of that ancient society and prominent personalities (e.g. Moses, Judah, King David) having married outside the faith, the priests couldn't and didn't add any law to the Bible forbidding intermarriage.

GOD CREATED HUMANKIND AND WANTED THEM TO MULTIPLY, but the Creation narrative says nothing about marriage.

> "So God created humankind in his image, in the image of God he created them; male and female he created them." (Genesis 1.27)

> "God blessed them, and God said to them, 'Be fruitful and multiply, and fill the earth ...' " (Genesis 1.28).

That was in the Creation narrative the priests added right at the beginning of the Bible. In the first Creation narrative that was written, the one that appeared in the first Bible before the priests made any additions, God is portrayed as having first created a man and then having created a woman, and nothing was said about being fruitful or multiplying.

> "... [T]he LORD God formed man from the dust of the ground, and breathed into his nostrils the breath of life; and the man became a living being. And the LORD GOD planted a garden in Eden, in the east; and there he put the man whom he had formed." (Genesis 2.7-8)
> "The LORD God took the man and put him in the garden of Eden to till it and kept it. (Genesis 2.15)

> [2.18]"Then the LORD God said, '... I will make him a helper .....' [2.19]So out of the ground the LORD God formed every animal .... [2.20] ... but for the man there was not found a helper ....[2.21] So the LORD God caused a deep sleep to fall upon the man, and he slept; then he took one of his ribs and closed up its place ....[2.22] And the rib that the LORD God had taken from the man he made into a woman..." (Genesis 2.18-22, first Bible text only, without the priests' additions)

41

The two Creation narratives are very different. The priests' Creation narrative was concerned with being fruitful and multiplying while the first Bible's Creation narrative was concerned with tilling the garden and made no reference to sex.

THE HUSBAND/WIFE CONCEPT IS INTRODUCED by the priests without mentioning the word "marriage." At the end of the above quoted first Bible's Creation narrative, after adding some text about bones and flesh, and naming the woman as woman and the man as man (whatever that is supposed to mean), the priests use the word "wife" and thereby introduced the husband/wife concept that was so important to them.

> **"Then the man said, 'This at last is bone of my bones and flesh of my flesh; this one shall be called Woman, for out of Man this one was taken.' "**
> **(Genesis 2.23)**

> **"Therefore a man leaves his father and mother and clings to his wife, and they become one flesh."**
> **(Genesis 2.24)**

So while there were only two people on earth, just one man and one woman, the priests already introduce talk of fathers and mothers, breaking the parental bond and clinging to wives. The man's clinging to the wife might relate to a maturing male leaving one's parents, but cannot relate to the first male, created by God and not born of parents. Nor do the priests mention how a woman's status as a wife is determined. If it implies marriage, the priests do not mention what marriage is, do not mention how the first two people on earth got married or anything else about marriage.

The priests had alluded to sex earlier when they added to the first Bible that God brought the woman to the man (Genesis 2.22). And the priests continued to insert wife and husband language into the first Bible's text way before the first sexual act had even taken place.[*]

All that can be said at this point is that the priests were setting the stage for what could be called their "natural law" reflecting a bias for marriage. There was then no law, natural or not, clearly stated in the Bible itself. Talking about a natural law is no more than speculation based on a personal view.

Of course, readers read with their own glasses. As they know of marriage and husbands and wives, they read that into the Bible, even though the narrative takes place at beginning of time when such concepts are premature and speculative.

What is meant by "clinging" is most vague. "Clinging" could refer to some sort of holding-on over time, but with divorce being allowed (e.g. Deuteronomy 24.3) there would be no permanence to it in the ancient society. With the availability of divorce to the male, at a minimum it would appear that there was no "clinging" to one woman unless the man chose to do so.

Nor would the clinging be "exclusive" as the Bible soon shows that a man could and did take more than one wife (Genesis 4.19). King Solomon had 700 wives (1 Kings 11.3) and his father King David had more than 7 wives (1 Samuel 18.27, 2 Samuel 3.3, 5.13). King Saul had only one wife (1 Samuel 14.50), Jacob had two wives (Genesis 29.21-28) and Gideon had many wives (Judges 31.29). All these personages (the first three kings of the nation, one Patriarch of the religion and a judge of the nation) also had concubines. And the distinction between a wife and a concubine was never made clear in the Bible.[†]

---

[*] The man first "knew" the woman in either Genesis 4.1 or 4.25 depending on a matter not relevant here. "Knowing" the woman is a euphemism for sexual intercourse.
[†] In the Jacob narrative, Jacob had two wives who gave their two maids (Bilhah and Zilpah) to Jacob as wives (Genesis 30.4, 30.9, 31.17), but in Genesis 35.22 Bilhah was called a concubine. In the Gibeah narrative, the woman is called a concubine (Judges 19.1-2) while the man was referred to as being her husband (Judges 19.3).

Men also used prostitutes (e.g., Genesis 38.15-16). Prostitution was apparently widespread as it was mentioned frequently in the Bible. It does seem that the ancient society was quite promiscuous.

With widespread prostitution, with the existence of concubines and with the many wives men could and did have, there could only be "one flesh" on a temporary or short term basis. So, aside from there being no clinging to one wife, there is no "one flesh" unless it is viewed serially as the man becomes "one flesh" with each wife (or concubine) as he has intercourse with them.

The talk about, and emphasis on, "flesh" is puzzling. It starts with God closing up the wound after the rib was taken. The priests added that the wound was closed "with flesh." That was a superfluous addition for it is not necessary to the narrative to know how God closed the wound. It is also unnecessary, for how else would the wound have been closed?

The purpose appears to be the introduction of the word "flesh" to the narrative so as to set the stage for the reference to "one flesh" during intercourse with one's wife. The implication could have been that the sexual act itself, intercourse, brought the rib[*] back together with the rest of the body. That would make for the "one flesh" and produce a complete being while intercourse lasted.

We can speculate as to the meaning of "one flesh," but we cannot insist on any particular reading. At best, it is unclear. At worst, it is just wrong. Perhaps the "one flesh" was meant to be fleeting or serial. Perhaps it extols the sexual act. It probably does

---

[*] In a fanciful view, the first man could be said to have been androgynous, possessing both male and female characteristics. This would have accorded with man being in God's likeness and God having both male and female attributes as some people believe. The extraction of the rib would be said to have separated out the female side so that the male and female sides would forever seek to reunite and become one again. Interestingly, this view would support the practice of cloning. God making woman out of man's rib could be viewed as cloning but for the change in gender, and man having an androgynous nature would support the gender change in cloning.

refer to marriage. We can speculate as to that, but we cannot insist that it mandates marriage.

There is nothing in the Bible that specifically mandates marriage. There is no commandment, law or ordinance that requires it. The existence of marriage is recognized as existing in the Bible but that itself does not mandate it. The Bible mentions slavery, but that does not mean the Bible mandates it.

In forbidding adultery, the commandments recognize the existence of marriage (Exodus 20.14). But it does not mean that a man with more than one wife is committing adultery. As a man can have many wives as well as concubines and not offend the commandments, it is difficult to bootstrap the prohibition of adultery into the requirement of marriage.

However, in two very limited circumstances the Bible does require the parties to marry.

A dead husband's brother is obligated to give the widowed wife a child so as to preserve his dead brother's name and inheritance (Deuteronomy 25.6). The brother must take the wife in marriage (called "levirate-marriage"); but if he doesn't, he faces nothing more than social disgrace (Deuteronomy 25.7-10).

Although the practice is called levirate "marriage," a child might be given the woman with no marriage taking place as was the case in the Judah/Tamar narrative (Genesis 38). The case for treating "levitate-marriage*" as an instance of compulsory marriage is weak because the circumstances are so narrow, because for the penalty for not marrying is slight, and because there was no marriage in the one instance the practice was portrayed in the Bible.

Another similarly weak case for marriage being required by the Bible arises when a man seduces an unengaged woman (Exodus 22.16, Deuteronomy 22.28). In addition to marrying her, the man

---

* The levirate-marriage practice would seem to run afoul of the law that forbids sex with your brother's wife (Leviticus 18.16). However, with the brother being dead, having sex with the brothers' widow might not be the same as having sex with the brother's wife. So it isn't clear that Leviticus forbids the levirate practice.

must make a specified monetary payment to the father. However, if the father refuses to allow his daughter to marry the man, the man must pay a different bride-price (Exodus 22.17). Thus, rather than requiring marriage, the Bible gives the father is given an option as to whether his daughter marries.

A later addition to the Bible plays down the monetary aspect, elevates the requirement of marriage and converts the "seduction" referred to in Exodus 22.16 into rape because force was used when the man "seized" the woman (Deuteronomy 22.28). The man was required to marry the woman. As he might thereafter rid himself of her by divorce, he was barred from divorcing her during his lifetime (Deuteronomy 22.29).

Thus, in the two very limited situations where the Bible could be viewed as requiring marriage, the circumstances are very limited and the penalties slight because serious violations invariably entail the death penalty. Rather, the two situations seem to focus on the preservation of inheritance and property rights.

Nothing can be found in the Bible that bars consensual intercourse with an unmarried and unengaged woman, virgin or not, with the prevalence of prostitution in the land supporting this being allowed.[*]

Yet, the ancient people did marry and that is reflected in many pages of the Bible. Nonetheless, marriage was not made compulsory by any commandment, law, ordinance or directive in the Bible. There is nothing to cite or quote as to this because it just isn't there.

So too with respect to polygamy. No commandment, law, ordinance or directive can be found referring to polygamy, to say

---

[*] A father profanes his daughter by making her a prostitute (Leviticus 19.29) but no penalty is levied for doing this, except that the daughter of a priest is to be put to death is she becomes a prostitute (Leviticus 21.9). Thus, except for a daughter of a priest, the Bible does not bar unmarried and unengaged woman from free-love or even prostitution as long as the father condones it.

nothing of barring it. The priests could easily have added such laws and directives to the Bible, but they didn't.

In terms of what is said and not said in the Bible, which is the sole focus of this book, marriage was not compulsory and not defined, and polygamy was not barred. With marriage not being defined in the Bible, there is nothing to say who may or may not be married.

What is not forbidden is or should be permissible. Yet, it would be fair to speculate that the priests would not have allowed marriage in those incestuous situations where sex is forbidden (see the chapter "*Forbidden Sex*"). However, that would not bear on what the Bible does and does not say. The Bible itself does not define marriage or state who might or might not get married.

Intermarriage

Intermarriage is not barred by the Bible, but the priests' additions to the first Bible rant against marrying outside the faith; against marrying the *other* or the foreigner. Surely, perpetuation of the religion could have been a basic purpose in barring intermarriage as marrying a person of a foreign faith could lead to the faithful adopting foreign gods. On the other hand, it could also bring others into the religion, so the purpose is unclear.

Separating the people from the *other* by creating exclusivity, another major theme of the priests, reduced the opportunities for intermarriage and helped the people build their own culture and improve self-esteem. A number of priestly additions to the first Bible contributed to creating exclusivity, although other purposes were also served by those additions. Exclusivity was created by deeming the people to be the Chosen People of God (e.g., Deuteronomy 7.6), requiring circumcision (Genesis 17.10), imposing dietary and purity laws (Leviticus 11 and 12) and even requiring day of rest (Sabbath) each week (Leviticus 23.3) while the *other* worked.

The priests' dietary laws did more than demonstrate that the people were different than their neighbors. The people could only eat those foods biblically deemed "clean" and prepared in specified ways (e.g., Leviticus 11, Deuteronomy 14.3-21). As the people needed access to the appropriate "clean" foods under the dietary laws, they tended to live near each other in areas where those foods could be obtained. With the food having to be prepared in certain ways, and with the people living near each other, they would tend to eat and socialize together. As a result, contact and intermarriage with the *other* would be reduced and so would intermarriage.

On the other hand, free travel in and out of neighboring lands seemed to be the order of the day and that would tend to increase the opportunities for intermarriage. For instance, Moses freely went from Egypt to Midian to live (Exodus 2.15) and Samson freely traveled through Philistine controlled lands (Judges 14.1) and both married the *other*; Moses married Zipporah, a Midianite (Exodus 2.21) and Samson married a Philistine (Judges 14.8).

Many more intermarriages are mentioned in the Bible. Moses and Samson had only one wife each and so did Judah, his wife being a Canaanite (Genesis 38.2). Other major personalities had many wives and they too intermarried with the *other*. King David married Maach, a Philistine (2 Samuel 3.3) and King Solomon intermarried widely as there were woman from many nations amongst his more than 700 wives (1 Kings 11.1-3).

With all these major personalities having intermarried, it is understandable why no commandment or other law had been added to the Bible forbidding intermarriage. But the priests did talk-down intermarriage, even being very direct about it, but never legislating.

"King Solomon loved many foreign woman along with the daughter of the Pharaoh; Ammonite, Edomite, Sidonian, and Hittite women, from the

nations concerning which the LORD had said to the Israelites, 'You shall not enter into marriage with them, neither shall they with you; for they will surely incline your heart to follow their gods'; Solomon clung to these in love." (1 Kings 11.1-2)

The statement is essentially a caution against marriage for the reason given. King Solomon had married the Pharaoh's daughter (1 Kings 3.1, 9.16) and presumably married the women from those other named nations. The quoted statement is similar to what Moses says (Deuteronomy 7.3-4), also making it look like a caution for a specified reason rather than a law. This approach can also be seen in the Ten Commandments, the one actually called the Ten Commandments in the Bible (Exodus 34.27), where God cautions the people not to enter in agreements with aliens lest it become a snare to adopt their gods (Exodus 34.12, 34.15).

Notwithstanding all this negativity directed at intermarriage, marriage to alien women captured in battle is expressly contemplated in the Bible (Deuteronomy 20.10-11), and thus the Bible can be viewed as specifically allowing intermarriage. This approval of intermarriage conflicts with the disapproval in Deuteronomy 7.3-4. And the disapproval expressed in Deuteronomy 7.4 was turned into a caution by showing that it was grounded on the fear that the children of such intermarriages could turn to other gods. Nevertheless, the statements in Deuteronomy are the statements of Moses, not the direct statements of God. Moses was not a lawgiver, God was. Moses was a prophet and messenger of God, as reliable as could be, but still not a lawgiver.

The priests' ranting against intermarriage reaches its zenith in the Baal of Peor narrative. When some local men began to have sexual relations with women of Moab, God orders the leaders impaled (Numbers 25.1-4). After one of the local men brought a Midianite women into the congregation, Phinehas pierced the two of them with one stroke of his spear (Numbers 25.7-8). Whether this suggests they were at the moment engaged in intercourse is irrelevant. Phinehas must have pleased God because God stopped the plague He apparently had sent against His own people (Numbers 25.8). The plague had killed 24,000 of His own people (Number 25.9), seemingly killing indiscriminately as plagues are not known to be selective, and nothing was said about sparing the innocent. Phinehas was also rewarded by God declaring him and his descendants to be priests in perpetuity (Numbers 25.12-13).

While there are a number of things amiss with this narrative, as exhibited by the switch from Moabite to Midianite women, they were probably due to editors combining a couple of narratives and not being able to change the basic texts. Nevertheless, the narrative shows the extent the priests disliked intermarriage. Consistent with this dislike, Ezra, himself a priest, treated intermarriage as a trespass (Ezra 10.10) and saw to it that all who married foreign woman were driven from the community (Ezra 10.44).

The priests' fuming against intermarriage started slowly with Abraham demanding that a non-Canaanite wife be found for his son Isaac (Genesis 24.3).

It accelerated when Aaron and Miriam, Moses' brother and sister, severely criticized Moses for having intermarried (Numbers 12.1). God came to Moses' defense, showing that intermarriage did not matter to God (Numbers 12.4-9). As it turned out, Moses' intermarriage did not matter as Moses continued in his role. Moses' grandson even became a priest in the tribe of Dan (Judges 18.30).

So too with respect to Absalom, King David's son by his Philistine wife, Maach (2 Samuel 3.3). Although Absalom was a child of intermarriage, he had much public support in challenging his father for the crown (2 Samuel 15.1-18.33); also showing that intermarriage did not matter to the people.

Divorce

Divorce was allowed, as clearly shown in the Bible (Deuteronomy 24.1). As the wife was essentially the property of the husband, he was free to cast her out of his house. With no rules or limitations stated in the Bible, divorce would appear to be optional to the husband with the wife having no say. The wife, as a chattel of the husband, would not have similar right to divorce the husband and none can be found in the Bible. The one benefit of receiving a written certificate of divorce, instead of merely being cast off by some informal action (like the husband casting black or white stone) or ritual not involving a writing, is that the woman would free to marry and be able to prove she is free.

If a divorced woman marries again and is divorced by her second husband, the first husband is barred from remarrying her because of the unfathomable rationale that the second husband defiled her (Deuteronomy 24.4). A priest is barred from marrying a divorced woman (Leviticus 21.7, 21.14). Interestingly, the independence of a divorced woman is recognized by treating her vows as binding (Leviticus 30.9) while a married woman's vows might be nullified by her husband (Leviticus 30.12) and a daughter's vows nullified by the father (Leviticus 30.5).

A husband who falsely accuses his wife of not being a virgin when he married her is forbidden to divorce her (Deuteronomy 22.19). A man who is forced to marry a virgin he violated cannot divorce her (Deuteronomy 22.29).

With divorce being given biblical recognition in many respects, divorce does not appear to have been just an incidental or rare occurrence in the ancient society. Divorce, like marriage, was never biblically defined.

Chapter Four

Homosexuality in the Bible

The Bible condemns a man who "lies with a male as with a woman" (Leviticus 18.22). The word "homosexual" appears nowhere in the Bible, but the biblical condemnation does refer to what we today would call homosexual. Male-male anal intercourse is clearly condemned but beyond that there is no plain indication as to what activities are condemned. Homosexual activity can consist of a great range of activities, anywhere from anal penetration and oral and manual sex to kissing, touching and anything else that might be done behind closed doors. Even male-male love and affection without sex might be viewed by some people as being homosexual.

As it turns out from the words of the Bible itself, the ancient male society was homosexual in large or significant part. It would be more accurate to call it "bisexual" because the men did sire children with their many wives and concubines. Since the focus of the priests was homosexuality, bisexuality is put aside and reference is made only to the homosexual side.

Oddly enough, while the Bible is not prudish about sex, euphemisms are frequently used and their meaning is usually context dependant. For instance, "knowing" and "uncovering nakedness" can refer to intercourse, while "nakedness" or "feet" can refer to genitalia.

The Bible refers only to male homosexuality and doesn't mention women lying with women or in any other way refer to lesbianism.* While the biblical references to homosexuality might conceivably be thought to also apply to lesbianism, there is nothing in the Bible to support that. The Bible never alludes to the existence of lesbianism or mentions female-female sexual activity. It does appear that lesbians get a biblical pass.

In addition to forbidding homosexuality, the Book of Leviticus forbids a host of other sexual relationships, most of which would today be called incestuous, with a couple of glaring omissions. That is covered in the chapter *"Forbidden Sex ."*

However, there is much more to the biblical story, and much more to be said about the biblical condemnation of homosexuality.

THE WIDESPREAD PRACTICE OF HOMOSEXUALITY throughout the ancient land is first portrayed in the Sodom and Gomorrah narrative. The narrative emphasizes that all the men of Sodom (except obviously for Lot) were homosexual.

> **"But before they [Lot's visitors] lay down, the men of the city, the men of Sodom, both young and old, all the people to the last man, surrounded the house; and they called to Lot, 'Where are the men who came to you tonight? Bring them out to us, so that we may know them.' " (Genesis 19.4-5)**

---

* The there is no way to say how prevalent lesbianism might have been in the land, except to note that husbands could have many wives in addition to concubines so wives might have sought another sexual outlet. Having sex with any male other than the husband was forbidden to wives at the penalty of death.

In addition to there being no biblical references to lesbianism, there are no biblical references to any other type of so-called "transgendered" persons.

That narrative was based on the earlier written* Gibeah narrative that portrays a similar story. The Gibeah narrative did not speak to the percentage of city's men who were pounding on the door for sex (Judges 19.22); it could have been all the men of the city or just part of them, although the tenor of the narrative indicates it was a sizable group or all the men.

> **"While they [the old man and the visitor] were enjoying themselves, the men of the city, a perverse lot, surrounded the house, and started pounding on the door. They said to the old man, the master of the house, 'Bring out the man who came to your house, so that we may have intercourse with him.' " (Judges 19.22).**

All the men of Sodom ("to the last man," for emphasis) being homosexual is consistent with homosexuality being commonplace throughout the ancient land. That would necessarily follow from the biblical text. Logic would also indicate that such a concentration of homosexuals in one place (in Sodom 100% except for Lot) could not have been so explicitly stated if it were far-fetched. It would have been unlikely for the priesthood's hierarchy to have approved that addition to the first Bible if homosexuality was not commonplace in the land. Congregations of lay believers would not have accepted the priestly addition if homosexuality were just random deviant behavior infrequently encountered. Merely mentioning the existence of such a concentration of homosexuality in a single city supports the existence of widespread homosexuality throughout the land, and there is also much more to support that.

---

* The Gibeah narrative is found in the first Bible, it having been carried down through oral transmissions that were recorded in the first Bible. Priestly additions to the first Bible were so voluminous that the Gibeah narrative is now found in the Book of Judges. The priests added their latter written Sodom and Gomorrah narrative to the Book of Genesis, so it now appears earlier in the Bible.

Support for homosexuality being widespread is also found in Sodom being described as a city, not merely as a campground for homosexuals. And it wasn't only the city of Sodom that God destroyed. God also destroyed the city of Gomorrah and other cities of the Plain (Genesis 19.17, 28, 29). Gibeah differed in that the city was situated in higher country, indicating that homosexuality was not somehow restricted to the Plain.

The purpose and role of Sodom and Gomorrah narrative is unclear because issues of inhospitality, implied use of force, and a society running amuck are blended in the narrative. There is much in the narrative that points to inhospitality or to communities running amuck rather that homosexuality as being at the core of the narrative. The same elements are present in the Gibeah narrative, but its purpose is clear since we know where the Gibeah narrative led. These and still other aspects are discussed in the Appendix: "*The Sodom and Gomorrah Narrative & The Gibeah Narrative.*"

THE EXISTENCE OF MALE TEMPLE PROSTITUTION indicates that homosexuality had been an accepted feature of the ancient society and confirms that homosexuality was widespread in the ancient days.

There are a number of biblical references to male prostitution in the Bible and the existence of male prostitutes was surely not for the benefit of women. The customers were undoubtedly males. Thus, the biblical references to male prostitution, more so when it takes place in a temple, become a clear and direct confirmation of widespread homosexuality.

In addition to there being female temple prostitutes (Genesis 38.21), the Bible shows that there were male temple prostitutes (1 Kings 14.24, 15.12, 22.46, 2 Kings 23.7). That both male and female temple prostitutes existed in the land is shown by the Deuteronomic law condemning both (Deuteronomy 23.17). As prostitution took place in the temple, it is a fair assumption that the priests who oversaw the temple had condoned it before the addition of the Deuteronomic law to the Bible that outlawed the practice. It was the practice of prostitution within the holy place, and the contribution of the fees or wages of prostitution to the holy place (Deuteronomy 23.18), that were forbidden. The practice of prostitution by either males or females was not forbidden.

Alongside temple prostitution, both male and female, prostitution outside the temple was also widespread as shown by the many times female prostitutes were mentioned in the Bible (the Judah/Tamar narrative in Genesis 38.15; the Conquest of Jericho narrative in Joshua 2.1; the Samson narrative in Judges 16.1; the two prostitutes fighting over a child in 1 Kings 3.15-28). But for present purposes, it was the male prostitution that confirms that homosexuality was commonplace throughout the land, presumably both within and outside the many holy places.

ANTHROPOLOGISTS AND HISTORIANS also show that homosexuality was prevalent in many primitive and ancient societies all over the world, so it wouldn't have been unusual for the people living in what would turn out to be the Promised Land to have also been homosexual. Such primitive and ancient homosexuality is well documented by the scientists, and more so when it came to the more modern societies like that of the Greeks and Romans. For instance, the ancient Greeks and Roman were known for pederasty, where higher class older men would anally penetrate lower class boys and younger men, including servants and slaves.

While much might be said about this, no anthropological or historical material is used in support of this book, neither in this chapter or elsewhere. Nor is any reference made to homosexuality being found as natural in animal societies, as established by other kinds of scientists. No external sources of any type are relied upon. This book relies upon and refers to the text of the Bible and only that. No external confirmation is sought as this book aims only at describing what the Bible says and doesn't say.

SPECIFIC INDICATIONS OF HOMOSEXUALITY in the ancient land are also to be found in the biblical story narratives. It becomes necessary to dig for these instances because the narratives would have been written without particularly addressing homosexuality. This arises because the biblical authors would understand the existence and prevalence of homosexuality in their society and would not need to specifically mention it, and the ancient readers would not need to be told about it. With the authors of the Bible being reserved in the way things are presented and expressed, as exhibited by their use of euphemisms, the need for what seems to be digging becomes apparent.

As a result of this situation, there might well be instances there the narrative gives no indication of homosexuality and yet it would exist. Of course, nothing could be said about such situation because we just do not know about them.

On the other side of the coin, some person will see homosexually in situations where homosexuality does not exist. All same-sex relationships may be seized upon, particularly those referring to one "favoring" or "loving" another male in the biblical narrative. And yet, it would not, for instance, have been unusual for a young male armor-bearer to be in a homosexual relationship with his master, and perhaps most were.

Much of this presumed homosexuality can be exhibited or denied by referring to confirmations external to the Bible, as for example the work of historians, but that is not the function of this book.

In this book, what matters is only what the Bible plainly says. Thus, digging within the four corners of the Bible is required. And it is also required that we disregard what is, or is thought to be, generally known. This is a difficult chore, but in the end it does help arrive at what the Bible does and does not actually say.

DAVID HAD A HOMOSEXUAL RELATIONSHIP with King Saul and with King Saul's son, Jonathan, as it appears from the plain words of the Bible. A strong case can be made that the Bible portrays David, the famous King David, as being homosexual.

King David's having a number of wives and children and his affair with Bathsheba show him to be bisexual, not exclusively homosexual. It is probable that most homosexuals of the age fit into such a bisexual pattern. However, the focus here is only on homosexual activity; on the homosexual side of King David that is portrayed in the Bible.

Both King Saul and King Saul's son Jonathan played roles in David's life before they were slain in war (1 Samuel 31.2-6) and lamented by David (2 Samuel 1.17). David's lament included the following clear and direct reference to homosexuality:

> **"I am distressed for you, my brother Jonathan; greatly beloved were you by me; your love to me was wonderful, passing the love of women." (2 Samuel 1.26)**

David and Jonathan had a close relationship but, without more, it cannot be said to have necessarily been sexual. Yet, David need not have mentioned a woman as the lament did not call for it, and, by so doing, David himself introduced sex into the biblical narrative by implying that his homosexual love with Jonathan was more wonderful than heterosexual love with a woman. The emphasis on love, wonderful love at that, belies a mere platonic relationship.

While this is meaningful in terms of showing that a homosexual relationship existed with Jonathan, nothing much can be made from King David later favoring Jonathan's son, Mephibosheth, by restoring to him his grandfather's lands (2 Samuel 9.7) after having killed everyone else of the house of Saul (2 Samuel 9.1). Other reasons could have accounted for this besides King David's love for Jonathan.

The Bible contains two very different stories about how David came into King Saul's life, which later editors (redactors) melded together with some success in order to get a smoother reading Bible. But the two stories are still in the Bible and can be recognized. The editors faced the consistently adhered to prohibition on eliminating or changing existing sacred text.

In one biblical story, King Saul accepted the suggestion of his servants and requested a lyre player (1 Samuel 16.16-17). A servant suggested David, a son of Jesse, and Jesse sent David upon King Saul's request (1 Samuel 16.18-20).

> **"And David came to Saul, and entered his service. Saul loved him greatly, and he became his armor-bearer." (1 Samuel 16.21)**
> **Saul sent to Jesse, saying, 'Let David remain in my service, for he has found favor in my sight.' " (1 Samuel 16.22)**

Armor-bearers, usually young men or boys, had a close relationship with their masters, perhaps a homosexual relationship. The word "favor" sometimes suggests intimacy. David had been said to be handsome (1 Samuel 16.12) and the emphasis on male beauty is sometimes viewed as a homosexual earmark. Considering all this, the story can be read in a homosexual context. That would suggest the existence of a sexual relationship between King Saul and David.

Translation of the Bible can be brought into question so as to take the matter further. The King James Version of the Bible (1 Samuel 16.21) added that when David came to Saul, David had "stood before him" a phase that was not found in the New Oxford Bible nor in the Jewish Publication Society Bible. The possible significance of this requires explanation.

The ancient written Hebrew was without vowels. The meaning of the written word could be very different if different vowels were intended (as in h<u>a</u>t verses h<u>o</u>t). This was not a problem when the language was orally spoken as the verbal emphasis in speaking supplied meaning in addition to the context supplying meaning.

If the vowel in the added written phrase were changed, it would indicate that David had an erection as he stood before King Saul instead of David merely standing before King Saul. That could be read as making David more desirable to King Saul in a homosexual way. Aside from this, the other biblical statements can also be painted with a homosexual brush. There is David being loved by King Saul, David being King Saul's armor-bearer and David having found favor in King Saul's sight. All this serves to suggest that King Saul did have a homosexual relationship with David, a relationship that possibly contributed to King Saul's later hatred as David developed a closer relationship with Jonathan.

In the other biblical story, King Saul sent for David when he heard about what David had said about Goliath's challenge (1 Samuel 17.31). David offered to go up against Goliath but King Saul said he was just a boy (1 Samuel 17.32-33). David persuaded King Saul to let him fight Goliath (1 Samuel 17.34-37) and it was only after David prevailed against Goliath (1 Samuel 17.48-51) that King Saul asked who David's father was (1 Samuel 17.58) and David responded. In the first biblical story, King Saul already knew that David was the son of Jesse.

"When David had finished speaking to Saul, the soul of Jonathan was bound to the soul of David, and Jonathan loved him as his own soul. Saul took him that day and would not let him return to his father's house. Then Jonathan made a covenant with David, because he loved him as his own soul. Jonathan stripped himself of the robe that he was wearing, and gave it to David, and his armor, and

even his sword and his bow and his belt." (1 Samuel 18.1-4)

King Saul "taking" David that day could be a very direct sexual statement, a euphemism like "knowing" a person. Or it could merely mean that King Saul took David under his protection, which would appear to be somewhat redundant with not letting David return to this father. Jonathan's love for David becomes apparent, and the references to the "soul" seem to add or detract nothing from that. Jonathan giving his royal accoutrements to David are clear love gifts.

> **"Saul spoke with his son Jonathan and with all his servants about killing David. But Saul's son Jonathan took great delight in David. Jonathan told David ... [about it]." (1 Samuel 19.1-2)**

Thereafter, Jonathan became the eyes and ears of David, braving his father's wrath because of his love for David.

> **"Jonathan made David swear again by his love for him; for he loved him as he loved his own life." (1 Samuel 20.17)**

King Saul became aware of what would effectively be his son's treachery and King Saul berated Jonathan because of it.

> **"Then Saul's anger was kindled against Jonathan. He said to him, 'You son of a perverse, rebellious woman! Do I not know that you have chosen the son of Jesse to your own shame and to the shame of your mother's nakedness? ....' " (1 Samuel 20.30)**

If everything that had happened between Jonathan and David just indicated brotherly love and friendship, nakedness would not have been mentioned and certainly not Jonathan's mother's nakedness. The reference to Jonathan's mother's nakedness is a sexual reference, and it serves to confirm that both King Saul and Jonathan had sexual relations with David.

Using the rationale of Leviticus 18, when David and King Saul "knew" each other (had intercourse) they had uncovered each other's nakedness. When David and Jonathan had intercourse, they uncovered each other's nakedness. Thus, through his sexual relations with David, Jonathan had uncovered the nakedness of his father, which is the nakedness of his mother (Leviticus 18.7).

The concept behind Leviticus is that having sex with a person is like having sex with someone that person had sex with -- uncovering the nakedness of the father, "which is" the nakedness of the mother (Leviticus 18.7). Jonathan, through having had sex with David who had sex with King Saul, became connected in shame to his mother's nakedness. There had to be some sort of sexual connection to bring Jonathan's mother's nakedness into the narrative.

" ... [T]hey kissed each other, and wept with each other; David wept the more." (1 Samuel 20.41)

This was the last meaningful biblical reference to the homosexual love between these personalities before they left each other.

Considering everything stated in the Bible, the Bible clearly portrayed a homosexual relationship between David and Jonathan and also one between David and King Saul. It is a relationship that should not be unexpected when placed within the context of the widespread homosexuality of the age.

WHETHER JOSEPH OR HIS FATHER JACOB WERE HOMOSEXUALS is not at all clear.

At first there is a weak allusion to homosexuality in the "female" robe Jacob made for Joseph, the long robe with sleeves that is sometimes called the robe of many colors (Genesis 37.3). The robe might have suggested the femininity of Joseph for such robes were worn in the ancient days by virgin daughters of kings (2 Samuel 13.18). However, such use of the robe appeared in a Book of Samuel, which addresses a time much later than the time of Jacob and Joseph found in the Book of Genesis. Thus, for all we know from the Bible itself there could have been no special meaning to the robe in the time of Jacob, it having later been adopted for royal virgin use. Thus, it is not clear that the robe itself has any special sexual meaning in this narrative.

So too with Jacob putting a sackcloth on his loins, his sexual organ, in addition to ripping his clothes (Genesis 37.34) when he was told Joseph was killed. Normally grief was expressed in ripping one's clothes, and sackcloth (garment material worn by mourners) was used in various ways. For instance, there is a reference to sackcloth being placed around one's waist, which would cover the loins, in a clearly non-sexual context (1 Kings 20.31-21). The significance of Jacob putting sackcloth on his loins is far from clear.

Although Joseph was handsome and good-looking, his beauty was not emphasized in the biblical narrative (Genesis 39.6). Emphasizing male beauty might be found in narratives portraying homosexuality, but in this case Joseph's beauty was only mentioned when a female tried to seduce him. Joseph refused the sexual advances of the captain of the guard's wife (Genesis 39.7-12), which does not bespeak of Joseph's homosexuality as much as his prudence.

Much can also be made of Joseph's rapid rise to power in Egypt, but there is nothing to particularly ascribe it to homosexual favors. Toward the end of the narrative, Jacob adopts Joseph's two sons as his own (Genesis 48.5). The grandfather adopting the grandsons as his own sons is unusual and the unusual can lead to all sorts of speculation, although it would be appear difficult to ascribe it to homosexuality in any way.

Although there might be people who are inclined to view the Joseph narrative as indicating homosexual relationships, digging in the biblical text does not confirm it. And so it would go in still other biblical narratives, yielding nothing in itself nor any additional support for homosexuality being so widespread in ancient times.

MALE BEAUTY IS REFERRED TO IN THE BIBLE much more frequently than female beauty, and in much more superlative terms. By and large, the Bible does not mention the looks of a character, indicating that it is either irrelevant or that the person was nothing special to look at. Superlatives were used only where it came to male beauty and then only with reference to certain personalities. Those superlatives could lead to suggestions of homosexuality.

There wasn't much interest in a woman's beauty except that it might have been mentioned where it played a role in the story; otherwise female beauty got passing mention or wasn't mentioned at all. Nothing said of a woman's beauty could lead to suggestions of lesbianism.

Sarah (Abraham's wife) was said to be beautiful (Genesis 12.13) and because of her beauty winds up in the Pharaoh's harem (Genesis 12.15). The married Bathsheba was said to be very beautiful (2 Samuel 11.2) and winds up in the bed of King David. Rebekah (Isaac's wife) was merely said to be very fair to look upon (Genesis 24.15), which had nothing to do with her tale of deception.

Jacob's first wife Leah had lovely eyes and his second wife Rachel was beautiful (Genesis 29.17).[*] Nothing was said of the beauty of Bilhah, the maid of Rachel given to Jacob as a wife

---

[*] This is one of the few cases where differences in translation were found, and fortunately it is inconsequential. Rachael was also said to be graceful according to the New Oxford Bible, but shapely according to the Jewish Publication Society Bible (the "Tanakh"). Leah either had lovely eyes (according to the New Oxford Bible) or weak eyes (according to JPS).

(Genesis 30.4); nothing said about the beauty of Zilpah, the maid of Leah given to Jacob as a wife (Genesis 30.9); and nothing was said about the beauty of Hagar, the Egyptian slave-girl given by Sarah to Abraham as a wife (Genesis 16.3).

Nothing was said of the beauty of Judah's Canaanite wife (Genesis 32.2), nor of Tamar who married one of Judah's sons (Genesis 30.6). Nothing was said of the beauty of Moses' Midianite wife Zipporah (Exodus 2.21).

Samson marries a Philistine, with nothing mentioned of her beauty (Judges 14.1-8), nor of the beauty of the prostitute Samson had sex with (Judges 16.1), nor of Delilah who Samson fell in love with (Judges 16.4). Nothing was said of the beauty of David's many wives [Michal (1 Samuel 18.27), Abigail (1 Samuel 25.42), Ahinoam (1 Samuel 25.43), Maacah, Haggith, Abital and Eglah (2 Samuel 3.3-5)], except for Bathsheba who he married after their adulterous affair (2 Samuel 11.27).

Tamar, King David's raped daughter, was said to be beautiful (2 Samuel 13.1) as was Tamar's niece who was also named Tamar (2 Samuel 14.27). In the other rape situation portrayed in the Bible, nothing was said of the beauty of Dinah, the raped daughter of Jacob (Genesis 34.2-3).

Nothing suggests the existence of lesbianism with respect to any of these women; and not just because of the absence of superlatives in describing female beauty.

Superlatives were found in a number of cases where male beauty was mentioned in the Bible. Pointedly, there wasn't enough consistency in this to connect biblical expressions of male beauty to the existence of homosexuality. Two sons of King David were, in superlative terms, said to be very handsome (Absalom, 2 Samuel 14.25, and Adonijah, 1 Kings 1.6). Nothing was said about the beauty of two other sons (Amnon and Solomon) who played important roles in the Bible. Yet there is nothing to suggest any of the four were homosexuals.

The suggestion of homosexuality being connected to male beauty arises with respect to the narratives about King Saul and King David. Before he became the first king, Saul was said to be the most handsome young man in the nation and stand taller than everyone else (1 Samuel 9.2), a truly superlative statement. David, as a young man, was said to be ruddy, have beautiful eyes and be handsome (1 Samuel 16.12); nice but not a superlative statement.

Based on the biblical text concerning male beauty, taken alone, there could be no implication of homosexuality. Those who tend to see homosexuality behind the mention of male beauty were likely influenced by the more direct biblical statements (previously discussed) that pointed to the homosexual relationships of King Saul and David. By themselves, the statements as to male beauty convey no sexual implications. This is also shown by the Bible saying nothing about the looks of Jonathan, who was also shown to have a sexual relationship with David.

Based on the biblical narratives themselves, the expressions of male beauty cannot be used as a homosexual earmark.

"LOVE" AND "FAVOR" as portrayed in the Bible can sometimes refer to sexual activity, including homosexual activity, instead of just being indications of friendship without sex. A person would normally look at these terms as indicating friendship, respect and the like; as in loving your neighbor. Yet, there are just too many references to sexual love in the Bible to completely ignore the possible homosexual connection.

"Favor," in biblical terms, is sometimes viewed as having homosexual connotations. Of course, you favor the one you love and no sexual implications necessarily arise. Sex might or might not be involved, which can only be determined from the context in which the word "favor" is used. Where nothing more is said, where the bible is silent on the matter, inferring homosexuality would be a personal innovation on the Bible, basically pure speculation.

Perhaps the connection between "favor" and homosexuality arose from King Saul finding favor in David (1 Samuel 16.22) and that Jonathan favored David (1 Samuel 20.3). With a sexual relationship known to exist, it is easy to work backwards and find the implication of homosexuality in a word normally used to indicate a like or preference based on any number of non-sexual reasons.

This is seen where Joseph, son of Jacob, could be cast as a homosexual by persons of the mind to do so. The Egyptian captain of the guard found favor in Joseph, and he put Joseph in charge of his household (Genesis 39.4). The chief jailer was made by God to find favor in Joseph, and he put Joseph in charge of the jail (Genesis 39.21). Thus, Joseph's rapid rise in Egypt would be attributed to the sexual "favor" in which the captain and the jailer held Joseph. However, the big move-up in Egypt was the Pharaoh effectively placing Joseph in charge of all Egypt (Genesis 40.40-41) and the Bible clearly said it was due to God and to Joseph's wisdom (Genesis 40.38-39), denying any homosexual "favor" or relationship.

"Love," in similar fashion depends on the context in which it is used for its meaning. In ancient society, "love" could be viewed as being analogous to loyalty, as where a subject loves the sovereign. But there is also love in the family context and in any number of other situations that has nothing to do with any sexual relations. However, where the sexual relationship is found to exist, love in the traditional sense might or might not exist. For instance, the sexual relationship could be based on lust. Thus, there is no necessary connection between "love" and sex, either heterosexual or homosexual.

THAT GOD, YAHWEH HIMSELF, IS HOMOSEXUAL is outlandish. Yet humans, both man and woman, were created in God's likeness and image (Genesis 1.26), so humans would be as God is -- and God would be as humans are, similar to the way

Michelangelo portrayed the images on the ceiling of the Sistine Chapel.

"Likeness" and "image" would be redundant if they both referred to the outer or physical appearance, so the reference to "likeness" could refer to the inner as contrasted to the outer. With God and humans having a similar internal "likeness" as they have a similar external "image," their personal natures and attributes should be similar. Similar, but not the same, allowing for a range of deviation as humans are so varied, and allowing for the greater powers of God.

Within this context, the homosexual argument could be made. The matter would appear to turn on whether homosexuality is within this range of human variation or whether it is an aberration not to be generally found. For example, being a cripple would be an aberration, but being male or female, or black or white would be within the normal range of human variation. As homosexuality was so widespread in the ancient days of the Bible, the homosexual argument could be made and it was made in the folklore of the age.

A contradictory argument could be made based on wording of the Creation narrative. At first God talks to the other gods in what appears to be a divine council and refers to both likeness and image. Then, when it comes to action, God refers only to image.

"Then God said, 'Let us make humankind in our image, according to our likeness; ...' " (Genesis 1.26)

"So God created humankind in his image, in the image of God he created them; male and female he created them." (Genesis 1.27)

As a result, the argument can be made that while God had considered making humankind according to His inner likeness as well as His outer image, God wound up making humankind just in His outer image. This view is as valid as the one previously indicated, which gave God and humans the same inner likeness. Perhaps the better argument is that God just created humankind in His outer image, which more closely follows the words of the Bible.

Be that as it may, there is nothing in the Bible as to God that could possibly be viewed as referring to homosexuality, or any other sexual aspect, including marriage or having children. Although the Canaanite god, El, had a wife or consort named Asherah[*] (Astarte), that could hardly carry over merely because the Canaanite word "El" became the Hebrew word for God.

Viewing God as being like the men He created, the ancients did flirt with that view that God had a wife or consort, but there is no indication, suggestion or allusion to God having any wife, consort or child in the Bible itself. The Bible does refer to the sons of God (Genesis 6.2), not as separate deities in their own right, but as the sons of the two humans God had created (Adam and Eve) -- the Bible waxing eloquent as the sons took the daughters when the people began to multiply (Genesis 6.1).

People who view things in homosexual terms could have a homosexual view of Jacob's wrestling with God (Genesis 32.24-26) as being a sexual assault by God and Jacob's wound as being inflicted by a rigorous sexual attack of that nature. This appears to be a forced reading with only the very strange and virtually inexplicable nature of the encounter itself providing any justification for seeking a sexual explanation.

In another strange and puzzling narrative found in the Bible, God must have or was about to attack Moses aiming to kill him (Exodus 4.24). Moses' wife Zipporah repels the attack (Exodus 4.25) in a way that makes God leave Moses alone (Exodus 4.26) and we are similarly left wondering what the narrative was all about.

---

[*] The Bible mentions Asherah a number of times, all in the context of being an alien god, like Baal; idols of which must be destroyed (e.g., 1 Kings 15.13) There is also mention of the "sacred pole," meaning "Asherah pole" (e.g., Exodus 34.13, Deuteronomy 16.21, Judges 6.25-30).

Why God would wrestle with Jacob and why God should attack Moses is not stated in the Bible so we are free to speculate or innovate on the Bible as we would. We can paint the scenes with a homosexual brush if we want to, but the Bible cannot be cited as support for any such view.

In the end, nothing can be found in the Bible in support any specific view about the sexual nature or sexual activity of God.

THE LAW, IN THE BOOK OF LEVITICUS, enters the picture to condemn homosexuality, with a penalty of death.

Leviticus is a book of law, parts of which were probably taken from the customs, traditions and secular law, if any, of the ancient community; supplemented, of course, by what the priests wanted to add. But, as we stick only to what the Bible says, we can only attribute to the ancient community what the Bible alone says about the ancient community.

As the Bible shows homosexuality as having been widespread in the ancient community, there would have been no custom, tradition or secular law barring homosexual conduct. So the condemnation of homosexuality must have originated with the priest or priests who made that addition to the first Bible.

The Book of Leviticus was one of the later additions to the Bible, probably added after the return from exile in Babylon in the 6th century BCE, some 2,500 years ago. And, as with the other books of the Bible, subsequent generations of priests added to what the previous generations had added. When the condemnation of homosexuality was added to the Bible remains unknown.

The laws of Leviticus do not have the status of the Ten Commandments (Exodus 20, 34), nor were they consented to by the people (Exodus 24.3, 24.7). The Ten Commandments received the "consent-of-the-governed," perhaps originating that concept.

Nevertheless, the laws of Leviticus are laws that must be obeyed, although believers might be selective in the laws they decide to follow. Such selectivity does not seem to apply to the Ten

Commandments. For example, Leviticus forbids the sowing of two kinds of seed in a field or wearing garments made of two different fibers (Leviticus 19.19). The soundness of the former as a matter of agricultural policy might be questioned by a farmer based on modern science and the crops involved. The latter is probably generally ignored, disregarded by all but the most pious, as different fibers in a garment are today commonplace.

When it comes to sexual matters, Leviticus has a near monopoly on the Bible although some matters get broader coverage. For example, Exodus has a provision concerning seduction of virgins (Exodus 20.16), which is also covered by in Deuteronomy with a slightly different law (Deuteronomy 22.28). The Book of Deuteronomy essentially restates the laws found elsewhere in the Bible, providing little new law -- and it speaks in the voice of Moses, not necessarily in the voice of God.

Many of the laws of the Bible are repeated in different places in the Bible but only in the Book of Leviticus is there found a condemnation of homosexuality, which might make it a "lesser" law in the eyes of some people.

> **"You shall not lie with a male as with a woman; it is an abomination." (Leviticus 18.22) [the law]**

> **"If a man lies with a male as with a woman, both of them have committed an abomination; they shall be put to death; their blood is upon them." (Leviticus 20.13) [the penalty]**

Leviticus also provides against bestiality, and the way the prohibition is expressed might have a bearing on the issue of homosexuality.

> **"You shall not have sexual relations with any animal and defile yourself with it, nor shall any**

woman give herself to an animal to have sexual relations with it: it is perversion. (Leviticus 18.23)

"If a man has sexual relations with an animal, he shall be put to death; and you shall kill the animal." (Leviticus 20.15)

"If a woman approaches any animal and has sexual relations with it, you shall kill the woman and the animal; they shall be put to death, their blood is upon them." (Leviticus 20.16)

In the case of bestiality, all sexual relations of any type with an animal are broadly condemned without defining what that includes. It surely does not contemplate petting your dog or even kissing your dog. It has to contemplate something more than that, something generally considered as being erotic or sexual, and that would certainly include penetration or being penetrated. Most important, it is a broad prohibition and it can include any combination of sexual activities within the scope of "sexual relations."

In the case of homosexuality, what is being condemned is not two men sharing a bed in order to only sleep through the night, as one might do in a crowed hotel. What is being barred could include all types of sexual relations even though that broad language was not used as it was in the case of bestiality. A man lying with a woman could entail all sorts of sexual activity and the words used in the Bible would allow for it. But, first and foremost, it obviously contemplates penetration with, in the male-male situation, the anus substituting for the vagina.

A man lying with a woman could also involve kissing, caressing, oral and manual manipulation and perhaps other activities. Thus, while the law could be aimed at male-male anal penetration and only that, the matter must be considered open for it could include other sexual activities because the biblical phraseology is broad enough to cover it.

The law is not only directed at the man who allows himself to be penetrated or treated like a woman. That would be the case if the purpose of the law was only to enforce gender differentiation by stopping a man acting as a woman. The law penalizes both the man being penetrated and the man doing the penetration, the one who caresses and the one who is being caressed.

It is noted that the law does not apply to female-female sexual relations. The law applies only in a male-male context. The priests who wrote Leviticus were certainly sophisticated and must have know what women could have been doing sexually, as exhibited by their knowing enough to specifically address female activity in terms of bestiality. Thus, whatever the range of female-female sexual activity, lesbians get a pass in Leviticus.

APPLYING LEVITICUS'S LAW in the modern era presents a number of problems.

Today, one might say that the law discriminatorily applies only to male homosexuals and not to female lesbians. It is also discriminatory in that it does not provide how the legal determination is to be made and whether it is on the same proof level as other sexual crimes. But, of course, it would seem unjust to apply modern day legal concepts to the ancient agrarian society. Thus it was okay for the Bible to discriminate and put-down woman, which was what the priests did. And it should also be okay for the Bible to discriminate against men in condemning their homosexuality and not doing anything about female lesbianism.

The other side of the same coin would make it unjust to apply ancient concepts in the modern context in situations where the ancient concepts cannot be followed or are inappropriate in modern society. We generally adhere to this. We make exceptions to the biblical laws all the time. We try not to discriminate against women. We no longer allow slavery. We don't follow the biblical sacrificial laws, which may be impossible to follow today, or don't follow the dietary and purity laws that conflict with present day scientific knowledge. We don't follow laws, like not wearing a garment made of two or more different fibers, which make no modern sense. And we don't follow laws that appear outlandish today, like killing a disobedient son (Deuteronomy 21.18-21) or applying the death penalty as frequently as Leviticus did.

It is clear that we do not today do many of the things contemplated or mandated by the Bible. Because of this, it becomes difficult to insist that one feature or another be followed. In modern terms, it would be like selective enforcement of our laws, which is not permitted as a matter of public policy. However, not everyone feels that way.

One theory of government is that government exists so that people do not harm each other. The point might be raised that homosexual activity between two consenting adults harms no one and thus the government should not be involved. But, again, not everyone feels that way.

And so it goes. We can all agree on the literal, but take one step beyond the plain meaning of the words of the Bible and there is disagreement.

This book focuses on what the Bible literally says and doesn't say. And the Bible does clearly say that a male should not lie with a male as with a woman. Thus the Bible literally condemns the homosexual relationship, and whatever sexual activities that relationship contemplates.

Chapter Five

The Sexual Act

The Bible faces sex squarely and is loaded with sexual activity, some of it unseemly. However, the Bible never delineates what constitutes acceptable sexual activity other than point to intercourse. Even there, the Bible is reserved; frequently using euphemisms like "knowing" the other party or "uncovering nakedness" to indicate intercourse.

THE PRUDISHNESS REFLECTED in the use of euphemisms is puzzling because the many authors of the Bible proved to be very savvy about sex.

On one occasion an author would speak directly about the man going into the woman and, on another occasion, that author or another one would speak indirectly about the man uncovering the woman's nakedness. But at all times, the authors refrained from graphically describing the sexual act.

The euphemisms themselves vary in several versions of the Bible. The different words used in translation continue to say the same thing but the words selected indicate that personal sensitivities could be involved.

For instance, the version of the Bible primarily used in this book, the New Oxford Bible, used the euphemism "know" in its Sodom and Gomorrah translation (Genesis 19.5) and used "intercourse" in its Gibeah translation (Judges 19.22). The Jewish Publication Society Bible used the term being "intimate" in both instances.* The New International Version Bible said the men of town wanted to "have sex" with the visitor(s) in both narratives. In the New King James Version Bible, the townsmen wanted to "know them carnally" in both instances. In the old King James Version Bible, the term "know" was used in both instances. All these Bibles used the most knowledgeable and expert translators and all the translators wind up saying the same thing using different euphemisms.

THE OTHER PARTY TO SEXUAL INTERCOURSE can be of the same gender, and the preceding chapter was devoted to the male-male relationship. The Bible does not refer to lesbianism, the female-female sexual relationship, although the priests undoubtedly knew that women were sexually active and that their husbands had many outlets (other wives, concubines, prostitutes, other men) that could leave them without a partner. As the penalty was death when wives consorted with other men, the alternate sexual outlet for the wives could well have been lesbianism even though the priests never mentioned the word or otherwise indicated they knew it existed.

Yet, the priests were savvy enough to forbid bestiality and to specifically forbid a woman from giving herself to an animal. So it becomes very possible if not probable that the priests were aware of the widespread existence of lesbianism and condoned it. Whatever

---

* The Jewish Schocken Bible covers only The Five Books of Moses (the Torah) and uses "know" in its Sodom and Gomorrah narrative. It does not cover the Gibeah narrative which is not in the Torah.

their reason, the priests expressly condemned homosexuality while their silence condoned lesbianism.

SEXUAL TERMINOLOGY developed over time. Today, referring to the men of Sodom as being homosexuals would not be as accurate as referring to them as "bisexuals" since they undoubtedly had wives and sired children in populating the city of Sodom. If lesbianism existed, as was most probable, the more accurate term for its practitioners would also be "bisexuals" as they were wives and mothers.

The term "sodomy" arose out of the Sodom and Gomorrah narrative and today refers to both anal and oral sex. There is no mention of oral sex (fellatio) anywhere in the Bible and a euphemism may have been used for anal sex. The euphemism for anal sex could have been to "lie with a male as with a woman" (Leviticus 18.22, 20.13), although that phraseology could well have been meant encompass the full range of sexual activities that a heterosexual couple would enter into.

The word "onanism" arose out of the Tamar/Judah narrative and now refers to coitus interruptus as Onan deliberately spilled his semen on the ground when he seemed to be doing his levirate-marriage duty to give Tamar a child (Genesis 38.). For those who might consider trans-dressing to be a sexual activity, or be an earmark of homosexuality (or lesbianism for that matter), a woman was forbidden to wear a man's apparel and a man was forbidden to wear a women's garment (Deuteronomy 22.5).

THE PURITY LAWS impacted sexual activity. Bodily discharges were viewed as being unclean, and that applied to the discharge of semen in the case of a male and menstrual blood in the case of a woman (Leviticus 15). These discharges made everything touched (e.g., clothes, sheets, chairs as well as skin) unclean, triggering a variety of required purification rituals.

Heterosexual intercourse resulting in the discharge of semen makes both the man and the woman unclean, requiring bathing in water (Leviticus 15.18). A nocturnal semen discharge, or one caused by masturbation, would make the man unclean and require purification bathing (Leviticus 15.2-3, 15.16). Similar rules would apply to the discharge of menstrual blood. Oral sex, both fellatio (male) and cunnilingus (female) involve bodily fluids and would probably run afoul of the purity laws.

While purification is required, the sexual act is not prohibited, whether it is intercourse, oral sex or masturbation. However, there is one exception, a meaningful one. Having intercourse with a woman during her menstrual period is forbidden (Leviticus 18.19) and the penalty for both the man and the woman is banishment (Leviticus 20.18), which can be fatal in a harsh environment.

SEXUAL DESIRE AND LUST are duly noted in the Bible. Sexual desire first appears in the punishment text the priests inserted into the Garden of Eden narrative. The priestly addition greatly increased the pain of childbirth while specifying that the wife's desire shall be for her husband (Genesis 3.16), which would lead her to more and more pain. Lust for a woman was exhibited in the rape narratives of Bible (e.g., Genesis 34, 2 Samuel 13) and in the biblical laws that address seduction of virgins (Exodus 22.16) and the use of force (Deuteronomy 22.28-29).

A woman could be a harlot or whore. A death penalty for "whoredom" appeared in the Bible (Genesis 38.34), although neither the scope of the crime nor anything else about it was ever described. Nothing was said about the about the promiscuity of men although its existence was obvious. The husband could and did have many wives, concubines, and access to prostitutes, while the wife was limited to only one husband and having sex only with him. Widows and the unmarried had more scope.

PROSTITUTION seemed commonplace, demonstrating the existence of widespread sexual activity outside the marriage bed. There were both female and male prostitutes, some even being temple prostitutes. The male prostitutes undoubtedly served only males. Male and female temple prostitution was outlawed and the gains of prostitution were refused as donations (Deuteronomy 23.17-18). The male temple prostitutes were eventually slaughtered (1 Kings 14.24, 15.12, 22.46, 2 Kings 23.7).

Fathers casting daughters into prostitution were frowned upon but not penalized (Leviticus 19.29), however, daughters of priests faced death if they became prostitutes (Leviticus 21.9). Otherwise, prostitution was accepted. Prostitutes were allowed to offer themselves on roadsides (Genesis 38.14-15). Prostitutes were allowed to use the judicial system (1 Kings 3.16). The son of a prostitute, Jephthah, was allowed to rise to the level of judge over the entire nation, the highest leadership level before the monarchy was established (Judges 11, 12.7). The Jericho prostitute, Rehab, was allowed to live when Jericho was totally destroyed, and she was honored for helping Joshua in the conquest of Jericho (Joshua 2, 6.22-25).

A VACILLATING BIBLICAL PORTRAYAL OF SEX developed over time as many generations of priests made additions to the first Bible and also added to the text previous generations of priests inserted. What was apparently acceptable at one time (e.g., temple prostitution) was condemned at another time. But sexual promiscuity did not change as men had more than one wife from the early biblical text (Genesis 4.19) to more than a 700 wives and concubines in the case of King Solomon (1 Kings 11.3). The Bible always portrayed a sexually active society.

Time and time again the priests spoke against intermarriage, but never outlawed it (see the chapter "*Marriage, Intermarriage and Divorce*"). The priests aimed at deterring sex with women of different tribes (e.g., Numbers 25.1-9) and Samson, a judge of the nation, showed that they weren't effective.

PROCREATIVE VERSES PLEASURABLE SEX never entered the biblical discourse. Sex was neither said to be pleasurable,* nor was sex limited to procreation. The husband "clinging" to the wife (Genesis 2.24) could be due to pleasurable sex, but it could also be attributable to other things. Conversely, there probably wouldn't have been as much "clinging" if sex were limited to procreation. Also, widespread prostitution denied procreative sex.

There was a biblical directive for males and females to be fruitful and multiply so as to fill the earth (Genesis 1.28) but there is nothing in the Bible that made such procreation the exclusive purpose of sex. And there are countless indications of non-procreative sex taking place in the Bible.

The only clear biblical reference to pleasurable sex was King David saying that Jonathan's love to him was wonderful, better than the love of women (2 Samuel 1.26); an obvious homosexual reference, but still a reference to pleasurable sex. Pleasurable sex might have been the purpose of releasing a man from army service for a year after he married; the stated purpose being that he be free to be happy with his new wife (Deuteronomy 24.5). Others might say the real purpose was procreation.

---

* Sarah had referred to sex as being pleasurable (Genesis 18.12), but laughingly so in order to express her belief that she couldn't have a child at her age.

Chapter Six

Forbidden Sex

Forbidden sex is sex with near kin (Leviticus 18.6), which appears to be a general rule aimed at forbidding incest even though the word "incest" never appears in the Bible. The Bible lists specific relationships that gave rise to the sexual prohibition, as shown in the table at the end of this chapter. What is not forbidden is permitted.

All the prohibitions are addressed to adult males, with one exception; a woman is told that she shall not give herself to an animal for sex (Leviticus 18.23b). Having sexual relations with any animal was prohibited and cursed (Exodus 22.19, Leviticus 18.23a, Deuteronomy 27.21) and seems to apply to both men and women. However, with the made adult usually being addressed in the Bible, it was probably thought necessary to also specifically address the bestiality prohibition to women. As indicated in the chapter *"Homosexuality in the Bible,"* lesbianism or female-female sex is not addressed in the Bible, and thus is not forbidden.

Biblical Sex

The applicable penalties are frequently found in separate provisions. Where something is forbidden and no penalty provided, the practice is obviously frowned upon but not considered serious enough to have a penalty for disobedience. The more serious violation generally attracts a death penalty, with lesser ones entailing exile from the community. However, in those ancient times in harsh deserts and wilderness, exile might lead to death.

SEX BETWEEN FATHERS AND DAUGHTERS OR BETWEEN FULL SIBLINGS was not specifically addressed, as shown in the table below. Those relationships are obviously incestuous and should be forbidden. The problem arises because the Bible neither defines "incest" nor uses the term. The Bible forbids sex in a roster of family relationships. Our calling those relationships "incestuous" does nothing to explain the two obvious omissions from that roster.

A second problem is that the Bible does not include a catch-all provision that would pull-in similar relationships. By giving such a specific, detailed list of forbidden sexual relationships, a general rule like forbidding sex with anyone near of kin (Leviticus 18.6) falls by the wayside. The specific controls the general. Besides, a general catch-all rule would have no practical effect as there wouldn't be specific penalties attached to it.

So, as outlandish as it might seem today, the omission of the father/daughter and brother/full-sister relationships from the forbidden sex roster could well have been deliberate. Those relationships are too close and too pervasive for them to have been excluded in error or by oversight.

The Bible does specifically forbid a grandfather from having sex with a granddaughter (Leviticus 18.10) and specifically forbids a brother from having sex with a half-sister (Leviticus 18.9). This suggests that the failure to mention the closer relationships (father/daughter and brother/full-sister) was deliberate. Also, no penalty appears in the Bible for grandfather/granddaughter sex.

84

Brother/half-sister sex involves only the lesser penalty of exile or exclusion (Leviticus 20.17), the less serious penalty.

With the more distant forbidden relationships attracting lesser or no penalties, the deliberate omission of the father/daughter and brother/full-sister relationships from the roster of forbidden relationships looks more pragmatic. Perhaps the omission was grounded on these parties usually living together in the same household where anything can and frequently does happen. Perhaps the omission was grounded on the father's property rights in his children, which was so absolute that he could even cast his daughter into prostitution or force his daughter to marry his son. Perhaps brother/full-sister sex was omitted to avoid tainting all of humanity necessarily born of Adam and Eve's children (discussed below).

However, all this speculation yields nothing definitive or meaningful. The story narratives in the Bible that address these situations would be more meaningful.

In the narrative concerning Lot and his daughters, Lot's daughters got Lot drunk so that they could have sex with him. The daughters feared there wouldn't be any other men around for them, and they wanted children (Genesis 19.31-36). Thus, there was father/daughter sex in the Bible, and there was no condemnation of it. Nothing negative was said or implied, other than what might have been implicit in mentioning that the children of this incident gave rise to two clans that would turn out to be enemies of Lot's clan (Genesis 19.36-38). Lot was unaware of what was happening because he was drunk.

Judah, also unaware of what was happening but for a different reason, had sex with his daughter-in-law in the Tamar/Judah narrative (Genesis 38). As in the narrative about Lot and his daughters, there was no mention of incest and no biblical condemnation. But, in contrast to the Lot narrative, there was no implication of an adverse outcome. Tamar had a child, Perez, who would be an ancestor of King David (Ruth 4.18-22). Sex with a daughter-in-law is specifically forbidden under the penalty of death

(Leviticus 18.15, 20.12), but perhaps the widow is not longer considered to be a daughter-in-law.[*]

There are no instances of brother/full-sister sex in the Bible. The closest was the Tamar Rape narrative where Amnon raped his half-sister Tamar. Other than triggering Tamar's full-brother's intent to revenge her rape, Amnon escaped any punishment. He was not punished by his father, King David, nor condemned to any penalty in the Bible. All that was said, said by Tamar, was that the rape would be vile (2 Samuel 13.12) and that Amnon would be considered a scoundrel (2 Samuel 13.13).

FORBIDDING SEX WITH THOSE OF OTHER FAITHS was never made into a distinct biblical prohibition. As shown in the chapter "*Marriage, Intermarriage and Divorce*," the priests ranted and raved against intermarriage and having sex with those of another faith, but never inserted a specific prohibition in the Bible. With so many major personalities having married outside the faith (e.g., Judah, Moses, King David), and with God having supported Moses when he was criticized for intermarrying (Numbers 12.1-9), the priesthood might have thought it inappropriate to add a clear-cut prohibition to the Bible.

MARRIAGE WAS FORBIDDEN in a few situations, but in only one situation was sex between the parties forbidden.

A daughter could inherit from her father only when the father had no sons or male relations (Numbers 27.8-11). The inheritance would normally include the tribal land owned by the father. The inheriting daughter was forbidden to marry anyone of a tribe other than her deceased husband's tribe because the land ownership would go to the new husband upon marriage, and thus fall into the hands of another tribe (Numbers 36.6-8). Although all the tribes were of the

---

[*] Death seems to remove the forbidden taint. For instances, a man is forbidden to take a woman and her sister only while both are alive (Leviticus 18.18).

faith, the land ownership was to be kept separate, tribe by tribe. Marriage was forbidden, but nothing was said about sex.

When a husband died without having a son, the intent was that a brother of the deceased husband gives her a son (in so-called "levirate-marriage") so as to preserve the name and property of the deceased (Deuteronomy 25.5-6). The wife was prohibited from marrying someone else, and the crime of whoredom limited sex.

Priests were forbidden to marry a widow, a divorced woman, a defiled woman, a prostitute or harlot, or virgins not of his own kin or his own people (Leviticus 21.14). Perhaps it meant that a priest could marry only virgin daughters of close relatives. But nothing was said about the priests being forbidden have more than one wife or forbidden to have sex with widows and the others.

THE FIRST SIN PORTRAYED IN THE BIBLE might have arisen from sexual relations between parties forbidden to have sex.

Of course, at the time the first sexual act took place, there were no laws in the Bible that specified what sexual relationships were acceptable and what sexual relationships were forbidden and thus sinful. So, to determine what the first sin was, we can either apply those future laws or use our personal value system.

The disobedience to God in the Garden of Eden is bypassed because the word "sin" was not used and God's forgiving actions confuse whether He viewed Adam and Eve's action as being sinful. God's compassion in not killing Adam and Eve as He said he would and His clothing them before sending them off into the world without constraints and unharmed does point to forgiveness.

Sexual intercourse between the man and the woman took place soon after Adam and Eve exited the garden. Since Adam and Eve were the only couple on earth, they must have given birth to a daughter for their first male offspring to copulate with in order for humanity to survive. This necessarily involves brother/sister sexual relations and brings up the specter of sinful forbidden sex.

An issue immediately arises as to whether the first sexual act between Adam and Eve resulted in the birth of Cain (Genesis 4.1) or in the birth of Seth (Genesis 4.25). There is much in the Cain and Abel narrative that shows that the narrative was written for a later age when the population was much greater; and that the later written narrative was moved-up within the Bible to the time of Adam and Eve, with editors making it fit and read smoothly.

Only that would explain why God felt it necessary to mark Cain so that nobody would kill him while he wandered the world (Genesis 4.15). Only Cain's parents then existed, so there would have been no one around to kill Cain. God's marking Cain would have been an empty gesture, not worthy of God, showing that the narrative had been written with reference to a later time when a much greater population existed and God marking Cain made sense.

Cain went on to build a city (Genesis 4.17) when there was no one on earth but Cain, Adam and Eve and the daughter they would necessarily have had because the narrative states that Cain then had a wife. But still, with only four people then being on earth, building a city would have been another empty gesture, as there wouldn't have been enough people to occupy it.

As the Bible said nothing about Adam and Eve then having a daughter, it is most likely that Cain had found his wife amongst the large population that existed when the Cain and Abel narrative first found its way into the Bible. It is for these and still more reasons that the Cain and Abel narrative could be treated as a later addition to the Bible, making Seth the only child of Adam and Eve when the Bible was originally written.

Seth was the child of Adam and Eve (Genesis 4.25) and the couple would have necessarily had to give birth to a daughter for Seth to have a child (Genesis 4.26). The Bible mentions that Adam did have daughters (Genesis 5.4). Thus Seth would have copulated with his sister.

The same would be said if Cain were treated as the first child of Adam and Eve, for then it would have been Cain copulating with his sister. The result is consistent. Adam and Eve necessarily had a female child and either Cain or Seth copulated and conceived with her and sent humankind on the way to populate the world. However, that would have resulted from the first sin being forbidden sex with one's full sister. This would take us into the area were the later written Book of Leviticus would be silent.

If that sexual act by Seth or Cain were considered sinful, it would pass to their children for no more than four generations according to the two sets of Ten Commandments (Exodus 20.5, 34.7) and restated twice (Numbers 14.18, Deuteronomy 5.9). Also, with Noah being blameless (Genesis 6.9), the sin of Seth or Cain was either not inherited by Noah, and his sons, or was no longer considered by God as being a taint. Noah's sons, without taint, repopulated the world (Genesis 9.19), and they had wives instead of sisters to copulate with.

AS THE FOLLOWING TABLE SHOWS, any adult male having sex with a married or engaged woman is subject to the death penalty. This applies whether the adult male is married, in which case it is adultery, or is unmarried and doesn't fit the definition of adultery. The limited prohibition of adultery in the Ten Commandments (Exodus 20.14) had been greatly expanded (Deuteronomy 22.22-27).

It wasn't as if the prohibition of adultery in the Ten Commandments was aimed preserving the marriage vows because there was no such implied vow on the part of the male since he could take more than one wife. Rather it appears that the property rights of the husband in the wife were being protected. An engaged woman was treated as being married because of the contractual aspects. But, once again, uncovering the rationale behind the law is speculative and the rationale irrelevant as this book is concerned only with what the plain words of the Bible literally say. The table summarizes what the Bible says.

Biblically Forbidden Intercourse With:		Penalty	
Father	Lev 18.7	Death	Lev 20.13
Father's wife	Lev 18.8, Deut 22.30	Death	Lev 20.11, Deut 22.22
Father's wife's daughter (half-sister)	Lev 18.11	Cut off/exile	Lev 20.17
Father's sister	Lev 18.12	Punishment/guilt	Lev 20.19
Father's brother	Lev 18.14	Death	Lev 20.13
		Death	Deut 22.22
Father's brother's wife	Lev 18.14	Die childless	Lev 20.20
Mother	Lev 18.7		
Mother's sister	Lev 18.13	Punishment/guilt	Lev 20.19
		Death	Deut 22.22
Mother's brother's wife		Die childless	Lev 20.20
Full sister			
Half sister	Lev 18.9	Cut off/exile	Lev 20.17
Daughter			
Granddaughter	Lev 18.10		
Son's wife	Lev 18.15	Death	Lev 20.12, Deut 22.22
		Death	Deut 22.22
Brother's wife (sister-in-law)	Lev 18.16	Die childless	Lev 20.21
		Death	Deut 22.22
Kinsman's wife	Lev 18.20	Die childless	Lev 20.21
Wife and her mother	Lev 18.17	Death	Lev 20.14
With a woman and her daughter	Lev 18.17	Death	Lev 20.14
With a woman and her granddaughter	Lev 18.17		
With a woman and her sister, when both are alive	Lev 18.18		
With a woman who is married or engaged to another man	Ex 20.14, in part	Death	Deut 22.22-27
With a woman who is menstating	Lev 18.19	Cut off/exile	Lev 20.18
With a man as with a woman	Lev 18.22	Death	Lev 20.13

Chapter Seven

Picking-and-Choosing What to Accept

As you read through this book, it must become obvious that
the Bible spoke to a different society than the one we have today,
and much of what the Bible presented is no longer germane. The
Bible spoke to an agrarian society, a very ancient one. The social
fabric of the society and the laws were very different from what they
are today.

The old priesthood and Temple no longer exists so the
biblical rituals and sacrifices cannot be conducted today. Much in
the Bible is inapplicable or inappropriate for our times. We no
longer have slavery. We no longer treat wives and daughters as
chattels to be bought, sold, cast into prostitution or divorced as the
husband or father wills. We do not put-down women as the ancients
did. We do not follow the biblical purity and dietary rules that don't
make any sense today or have no science behind them. Woman are
not ignored and they can now freely own, inherit and pass-on
property, vote and hold office, and also receive equal pay.
Disobedient sons are not killed. We might work on the Sabbath
without fearing death.

The sexual mores of society have also changed. Men do not have more than one wife and do not have harems full of concubines. Menstruating women might or might not be avoided. Prostitution has been made illegal. We intermarry at will. Women now dress in "mens" slacks. We all use fabrics made of more than one fiber.

In addition to not following so many of the sexual mandates in the Bible, there are a host of other laws in the Bible that are generally accepted as no longer appropriate in modern society. Perhaps, the best known is the biblical law that requires an eye for an eye, a tooth for a tooth and a fracture for a fracture (Leviticus 24.19-20). When we get hurt, few of us today would demand an eye for an-eye and the like.

TRUE BELIEVERS IN THE FAITH can and do pick-and-choose what to follow in the Bible. It is a common practice of believers of all persuasions, from the most pious to the most lax. In so doing they declare what is and is not compelling for themselves, and few would feel they are doing wrong in the eyes of God. God Himself chose not to follow what He previously said He would do, as shown in His not killing Adam and Eve the day they ate the forbidden fruit. With this precedent, even the most pious can take comfort in their picking-and-choosing.

Believers pick-and-chose for themselves based on a number of rationales. Most likely, many feel that the rules they choose not to follow cannot possibly be applied today because society changed so much. Some would feel that the rules they disregard are merely inappropriate for modern society. Some would disregard rules that made no sense to them. Some might disregard rules that they considered spurious, not possibly inspired by God.

IT IS IN SUPPORT OF THE FAITH, not a denial of faith, when a believer picks-and chooses for herself or himself. If reason rebels against following particular biblical text, the theologian and philosopher Maimonides pointed out that the believer is faced with either denying reason or denying the Bible. However, following reason does not require denial of the Bible. Following reason just entails disregarding the offending text by picking-and-choosing. This allows wholehearted acceptance of the rest of the Bible, which is far better than denying the Bible.

THERE IS NO ONE AMONG US who has not picked-and-chosen in some fashion. As we do it for ourselves, we should expect and accept that others will do it for themselves.

Appendix

The Sodom and Gomorrah Narrative
&
The Gibeah Narrative

Nothing has more notoriety when it comes to biblical sex than the Sodom and Gomorrah narrative. But few people realize that there are two narratives in the Bible that deal with intended homosexual gang-rape of male visitors to a community.

The Gibeah narrative was written first, it appearing in the writings of the first author of the Bible. That was the author who first reduced the orally transmitted religion to writing, which writing necessarily amounted to the first Bible. The Gibeah narrative takes place after the conquest of the Promised Land, just before the establishment of the monarchy. So much was added by the priests to the first Bible that the Gibeah narrative appears in today's Bible all the way back in the Book of Judges (Judges 19).

The Sodom and Gomorrah narrative was an addition made by the priests centuries after the first Bible was written. It was inserted in the first Bible text covering a much earlier time, the time of

Abraham, so it appears in today's Bible in the Book of Genesis (Genesis 18-19). The Gibeah narrative is little known, perhaps because so much emphasis has been placed on the first five books of the Bible (the Torah or Pentateuch) which contains the Book of Genesis and not the Book of Judges.

In this chapter, the meaning of the Sodom and Gomorrah narrative will be first explored, then the Gibeah narrative. The focus here is just on the narratives themselves. The chapter *"Homosexuality in the Bible"* contains a much more extensive exploration of homosexuality.

Sodom and Gomorrah

Abraham looks up from his tent and sees three men (Genesis 18.1-2). As it turns out from the remainder of the narrative, the three men were God and two angels in disguise. Abraham welcomes them and feeds them a meal under a nearby tree (Genesis 18.3-8). After the meal, the three set out toward Sodom and God decided to tell Abraham that He intended to check out the outcry He heard against Sodom and Gomorrah for He, God, did not know how grave their sin was (Genesis 18.16-21).

The two men proceeded to Sodom while Abraham and God remained behind to talk (Genesis 18.22). This is when Abraham engaged in his famous cross-examination of God's willingness to destroy the righteous along with the wicked, God conceding that He would not destroy Sodom if 10 righteous men could be found there (Genesis 18.23-32). Afterwards, God went off and Abraham returned to his tent (Genesis 18.33).

The two men were invited by Lot, Abraham's nephew who lived in Sodom with his wife and two daughters, to be guests in his house and Lot fed them (Genesis 19.1-3).

> **"But before they lay down, the men of the city, the men of Sodom both young and old, all the people to the last man, surrounded the house; and they called to Lot, 'Where are the men who came to you tonight? Bring them out to us, so that we may know them.' "** (Genesis 19.4-5)

Instead, Lot offered the men of Sodom his two virgin daughters, pleading that nothing be done to the men as they were his guests under his roof (Genesis 19.6-8). The two men, the angels in disguise, kept the men of Sodom from entering Lot's house. Later, the angels helped Lot to flee with his family before God, through the angels, rained sulfur and fire on both Sodom and Gomorrah, and on other cities of the Plain, destroying those cities and all their inhabitants (Genesis 19.10-25).

While it is clear that God destroyed Sodom and Gomorrah because of the great outcry of against those cities, and that their sin must have indeed been grave (Genesis 18.20) for God to do so, the biblical narrative never addresses the nature of the grave sin.

The men of Sodom wanted to "know" (Genesis 19.5) the visitors, a term generally conceded to mean "intercourse." The Gibeah narrative, the narrative on which the Sodom and Gomorrah story was obviously based, used the direct term "intercourse" (Judges 19.22), which could indicate that the euphemistically indirect word "know" meant something less than intercourse in the Sodom and Gomorrah narrative. This is a difficult argument to make because there are many, many instances in the Bible where the term "know" is clearly used to mean intercourse, the first such use being in the Adam and Eve narrative (Genesis 4.1 or Genesis 4.25).

We can reasonably accept that the men of Sodom wanted to have intercourse, homosexual intercourse, with Lot's male guests and we can also accept that it would be involuntary, or homosexual gang-rape. At this point, one might say that the "sin" (the grave sin referred to in Genesis 18.20[*]) related to rape, to the use of force, to the involuntary nature of sexual activity without consent.

However, it is also possible that neither homosexuality nor the use of force was the grave sin God ultimately acted upon. The grave sin could have been the communal breach of hospitality. Each of these possibilities (homosexuality, use of force, and inhospitality) will be examined as they seem to be the popular rationales for the Sodom and Gomorrah narrative. To this, still another rationale is added: that of a community running amuck.

HOMOSEXUAL and not heterosexual rape was potentially involved in the Sodom and Gomorrah narrative. In that age the treatment of men and women was so dissimilar that it would be difficult to explore what the narrative would have stood for if, instead of men being the guests, Lot's guests were woman and heterosexual rape was in store. One might well speculate that the unsavory way the men of Sodom acted would still be considered sinful whether heterosexual or homosexual rape were involved. While this is pure speculation, such a reading would eliminate homosexuality from being the sin that lead to the destruction of Sodom and Gomorrah. The Gibeah narrative would lend support as the rape that did take place in Gibeah was heterosexual rape.

Both the Sodom and Gomorrah and Gibeah narratives point to homosexuality being widespread in the ancient land, and in neither narrative was there a specifically stated condemnation of homosexuality. Homosexuality being widespread in the land is shown in the Sodom and Gomorrah narrative emphasizing that every man (young and old to the last man) of Sodom was a homosexual, all of them being at Lot's door demanding homosexual sex (Genesis 19.4). Such conformity, 100% of the men being homosexual,, would

---

[*] This is the only mention of the word "sin" in the entire Sodom and Gomorrah narrative. The word "sin" was also mentioned when Lot first moved to Sodom (Genesis 13.13) so as to set the stage for this narrative, the men of Sodom then being called wicked sinners.

be inconceivable if homosexuality were just deviant behavior not frequently found in the land.

The Gibeah narrative doesn't go as far as the Sodom and Gomorrah narrative because Gibeah does not state that all the men of the city, to the last man, demanded intercourse with the male guest. The Gibeah narrative refers only to the men of the city without quantifying how many turned out, although there was a sufficient number to surround the house (Judges 19.22). While a person could read the Gibeah narrative as though all the men of the Gibeah turned out at the door demanding homosexual intercourse, that would be speculative since it was not plainly stated in the Bible. However, the phraseology used (the men of the city) does not appear to refer to just a select few, but does seem to suggest that a fair number of the men of Gibeah could have been homosexual.

If homosexuality had been the grave sin God found to exist in Sodom (Genesis 18.20), it would stand out that God did nothing to rid the rest of the land of homosexuals. There wasn't even a verbal condemnation of homosexuality in the Sodom and Gomorrah narrative. If homosexuality had been the sought grave sin, one might have expected God to have done something to rid the land of it or at least condemn it.

A person might say that the priests went overboard in showing that there weren't 10 righteous men in Sodom so that there would be no doubt that God fulfilled the commitment He gave to Abraham (Genesis 18.32). Showing that every man in the city to the last man (other than Lot) was wicked could have been excessive exuberance on the part of the priest who wrote it. Yet, it is unlikely that such exuberant text, if it was merely that, would have received the approval of the priestly hierarchy to add that text to the Bible, and also unlikely for that text to have been accepted by lay believers if homosexuality wasn't then commonplace in the land.

It would seem that the men of Sodom were bisexual and not strictly homosexual. Sodom was said to be a city, connoting a population that included women and children, and not merely a meeting place for homosexuals. Lot did live there with his wife and daughters. Saying that there could have been at least 10 righteous men in the city because there must have been enough heterosexual men (exclusively heterosexual men) to populate the city would be the most speculative and fly in the face of the actual narrative which points to all of the men being homosexual or bisexual.

Lot's two daughters were engaged to men of Sodom (Genesis 19.14), also indicating that the men of the city would be bisexual. Yet the Bible does not recognize the distinction between homosexuality and bisexuality. The Bible doesn't even use the word "bisexual." The Bible just focuses on the homosexual side and thus a bisexual male would be cast as a homosexual.

Lot voluntarily moved his tent to Sodom (Genesis 13.12) when he separated from Abraham so that their herds would have enough land to support them. At that point, the Bible volunteered the statement that Sodom was a wicked city (Genesis 13.13), calling the people there great sinners against the LORD. This statement was obviously made to set the stage for Sodom's later destruction, otherwise there would have been no reason to then mention that Sodom was a wicked city.

Lot might not have known that Sodom was a wicked place when he moved there, but once there could have moved on if he had found it uninhabitable. At that point, there was no mention of homosexuality or the euphemism for homosexuality (lying "with a male as with a woman") in the Bible.

The only specific condemnation of homosexuality in the Bible awaited the addition of the Book of Leviticus to the first Bible. We can speculate whether there would have been a specific condemnation of homosexuality in the Sodom and Gomorrah narrative had the condemnation of homosexuality (Leviticus 18.22, 20.13) then been in the Bible, but speculation yields us nothing.

At this point, all that can reasonably be said about homosexuality with respect to the Sodom and Gomorrah narrative is that homosexuality appeared widespread in biblical times, that there was then no specific condemnation of homosexuality in the Bible, and that the grave sin that God was seeking to confirm might not have been homosexuality. The grave sin could well have been something else, as the Bible itself shows that there were undeniable alternative rationales for the destruction of Sodom and Gomorrah.

USE OF FORCE, the lack of consent, the involuntary nature of the proposed rape could have been the grave sin that God was seeking to confirm. However, as with homosexuality, there is no clear indication whether a history of rape or multiple rapes could have been the grave sin of Sodom (Genesis 18.20) that led to its destruction. In the two rape narratives in the Bible, that of Dinah (Genesis 34) and Tamar (2 Samuel 13), the references were to seizure (Genesis 34.2) and the use of force (2 Samuel 13.14). In neither case was the defiling of the women called sinful or criminal. All that was said was that it was an outrage that ought not have been done (Genesis 34.7) or that it would be vile, not to be done in the land, and be an act of a scoundrel (2 Samuel 13.12-13).

In the Sodom and Gomorrah narrative, Lot offered his daughters up to the men of Sodom instead of yielding his guests to them.

> **"Lot went out the door to the men, shut the door after him, and said, 'I beg of you not to act so wickedly. Look, I have two daughters who have not known a man; let me bring them out to you, and do to them as you please; only do nothing to these men, for they have come under the shelter of my roof.' " (Genesis 18.6-8)**

As Lot would effectively substitute heterosexual rape for homosexual rape, Lot was not objecting to the use of force per se. Neither can it be said that Lot was concerned with homosexuality, because Lot did not mention homosexuality nor distinguish between homosexual and heterosexual rape but Lot did specifically refer to hospitality; ostensibly, the breach of hospitality was important to Lot, not the use of force.

THE VIOLATION OF HOSPITALITY was Lot's concern, not the homosexuality of the men of Sodom. Lot pleaded only that nothing be done to the men who were his guests, and gave hospitality as the grounds for his plea (Genesis 18.8). His plea was expressly based on the men being Lot's guests, their having come under the shelter of Lot's roof. Thus, based on the words used by Lot, words that contained the sole expression of concern, it was only the breech of his hospitality that concerned Lot.

Lot had been willing to offer-up his daughters so as to protect his guests, and that would have been costly to Lot. Lot's daughters would have produced bride-prices for him as they were engaged to two local men (Genesis 19.14). Had the men of Sodom accepted Lot's offer of his daughters, Lot would likely have had to refund the bride-prices if he had already received them and be saddled with the future support of his unmarriageable, raped daughters.

Yet, it must be recognized that Lot could have been so protective of his guests because he recognized them as divine beings,* angels, as witness his bowing to them with his face touching the ground at the gate of Sodom (Genesis 19.1). Thus, Lot had known that the physical male appearance of his guests was a disguise, and while possibly not knowing the extent of angels' powers, he invited them into his house as guests and fed them (Genesis 19.2-3).

---

* Abraham also recognized this as he had bowed all the way to the ground when he first saw the three men (Genesis 18.2), indicating that Abraham also thought he was in the presence of divine beings. Other indications that the three were divine beings were their sudden appearance (Genesis 18.2) and the text continuing to shift back and forth between the three being men, angels and God. There was the shift from the men talking (Genesis 18.5) to God talking (Genesis 18.13); the shift back to the men walking (Genesis 18.16); the shift back again to God talking (Genesis 18.17-21); the shift to the men walking toward Sodom while Abraham spoke with God (Genesis 18.22) , and finally the shift to the two angels reaching Sodom (Genesis 19.1) but still retaining their disguise as men (Genesis 19.10).

We can speculate as to why Lot invited them in, and to why the angels would have accepted. We can also speculate as to why Lot should have been so concerned with the threatened rape of angels; whether rape was even possible considering the powers the angels had and later exhibited. Yet, this is the way the story added by the priests unfolded. But still, the only unequivocal and specifically stated rationale found in the plain words of the Bible was that guests weren't to be harmed because they were guests.

A SOCIETY RUNNING AMUCK is often said to arise where there is no religion; that is, it is religion that keeps societies from running amuck. Yet, law and order can exist without religion where the community's traditions and customs provide the restraints otherwise provided by religion.

However the restraints are provided, we all rebel against a community running amuck and perhaps that is what repels us in the Sodom and Gomorrah narrative. We do not like what happened there. We are appalled by it. So we seek rationales to condemn it even though there is no single rationale that can find clear support in the Bible.

Perhaps the rationale is as simple as just being revolted by what was going on there, a society running amuck. Simply put, the Sodomites were punished for their bad behavior, or, in priestly holiness terms, for their grave sinful behavior.

It is not a story of punishment and reward for it is difficult to view Lot's uprooting as a reward to him. It is not a reward for Lot being righteous, which is denied by his offering up his daughters. It is more of a story of God asserting His power to create the world He wants.

WHAT IS AMISS WITH THE SODOM AND GOMORRAH NARRATIVE? Plenty. The issues now presented are very different from those previously presented. The matters already discussed are now put aside and the narrative is examined from another viewpoint, which leads to issues about the fundamental justification for God having destroyed Sodom and Gomorrah.

The Sodom and Gomorrah narrative is examined from the viewpoint of the time and place the narrative is found in the Bible. That is, the Sodom and Gomorrah narrative was written by priests who placed the narrative at the time of Abraham, so the narrative is examined in the context of the age of Abraham.

THE NEW RELIGION DID NOT YET EXIST AND THE MEN OF SODOM SHOULDN'T BE JUDGED AS THOUGH THEY WERE BELIEVERS. The Sodom and Gomorrah narrative takes place at the time of Abraham when the new religion was just starting. At that time it would be hard to say that a religious belief system even existed.

God had just become the God to Abraham and his offspring (Genesis 17.7), then consisting only of Ishmael. There was also Sarah and Lot[*] who might also be counted for this purpose, but still there would be less than a handful.

A case can be made that the religion hadn't yet come into existence, not only because there were so few believers. To be sure, God had said that He would establish a covenant with Abraham and be God to Abraham and his offspring (Genesis 17.7), but no belief system was yet specified.

And, as yet, there hadn't even been any clear indication that this handful of people believed in God. It isn't even clear that Abraham himself believed for he did then express his doubts by laughing to himself when God told him that he would have a child at

---

[*] It is not clear when Lot married and had his daughters. At the time Abraham left his family to go to Canaan, he took only Sarah and Lot (Genesis 12.5) with him. There was no mention of Lot having a wife. After Abraham took Lot back from his side trip to Egypt (Genesis 13.1), Lot settled in Sodom (Genesis 13.12), Lot was captured (Genesis 14.12) and later freed (Genesis 14.16) and still there was no mention of a wife, to say nothing of daughters. It would appear that Lot found a wife while he was living in Sodom and had his daughters there.

his age (Genesis 17.17). Before then, Abraham had questioned God a number of times.*

Much time passed before it could be said that there was a people who believed in God. When Jacob and his family entered Egypt they numbered 70 persons, excluding the wives of Jacob's sons (Genesis 46.26-27). Thus, no more than 100 believers in this new religion existed generations after Sodom was destroyed.

Yet, the priests were judging and condemning non-believing Sodomites who had no connection with God or the new religion. The world was then populated by many different peoples with Sodom and Gomorrah being only a small part (and with Abraham and his offspring hardly being a people). Those peoples had their own customs and traditions and undoubtedly had their own gods. They probably knew nothing of God and the new religion.

In that obviously polytheist age, there were many peoples with each having their own gods. These peoples lived near each other, had friendly relations with one another, and even welcomed strangers. Abraham himself was a stranger allowed to live in an alien land. Sometimes these peoples went to war with one another, but it did not seem that a god would sit in judgment of the righteousness of another people having another god.

Nor is it clear as to who was being protected in the Sodom and Gomorrah narrative. Lot and his family were apparently getting along with the local people, and his daughters were engaged to marry two of them. It couldn't have been God's own angels who were being protected as angels need no protection, can fend for themselves and might even be viewed as having triggered the entire

---

* After the first time Abraham questioned God (Genesis 15.2-3), the Bible specifically stated that Abraham "believed"(Genesis 15.6), a very unusual statement. Thereafter Abraham goes on to again question God; that is, how was he, Abraham, to know whether he will ever possess the land God promised him (Genesis 15.8)? Not taking God at His word doesn't speak of belief. Still later, in the Sodom and Gomorrah narrative itself, Abraham questioned whether God was just (Genesis 18.23-25). And this says nothing about Abraham laughing at what God told him (Genesis 17.17), and Sarah also laughing at God (Genesis 18.12-15).

matter. That is, had the angels not gone to Sodom, it is not apparent that anything would have happened. Lot's engaged daughters would have married and life would have gone on. It wasn't that Sodom was un-inhabitable by decent people for Lot did choose to settle there, marry there, and have children there.

A later priestly addition to the first Bible, an obviously muddled one, seems to show Sodomites as being believers in the new religion. It reads as thought God destroyed Sodom in anger because the people there [the Sodomites] abandoned the covenant of God which their ancestors brought out of Egypt (Deuteronomy 29.23-25). Putting that aside as being poorly written or translated, an earlier priestly addition to the Bible is much more troublesome.

That addition shows the Sodomites as being disloyal to the God of Abraham, a God they didn't even know. The Sodomites were called "great sinners against the LORD" (Genesis 13.13). It is as if the priests believed that LORD, whose people were just Abraham and less than a handful of others, was LORD to all the peoples of the world.

Needless to say, the Bible recognizes time and time again that God had His own people, the Chosen People, and that there were other peoples with other gods; which the Bible could label as false gods, but still recognize that those people did not believe in the LORD God. Nowhere else, nowhere other that in the Sodom and Gomorrah narrative, is a foreign people treated as though they had been believers.

Thus, the rationale for God judging another people, the Sodomites, is not at all clear. When the Sodom and Gomorrah narrative is considered within the context of the time it appeared in the Bible, it doesn't so much raise questions as to homosexuality, involuntariness or inhospitality as it does to the fundamental justification for God destroying the city. Yet, this is the way the priests wrote their narrative.

AT THE TIME OF ABRAHAM, GOD HADN'T YET MADE HIS LAWS KNOWN. "Sin" is disobedience to God, not merely bad conduct.* At the time of the Sodom and Gomorrah narrative, God hadn't yet given His commandments, laws and ordinances. So it couldn't then be said what God wanted. That awaited the exodus from Egypt, after which God issued His commandments (Exodus 20, 34), followed by God's other laws and ordinances. It was at that point in time when it first became known what God wanted and demanded, and only then could "sin" exist.

Thus, it is difficult to say that the destruction of Sodom was based on God's law and thus "sinful," to say nothing of the grave sin the priests said God was trying to ascertain (Genesis 18.20-21).

Even if we assume that the laws of Moses existed (in mind or thought if not in writing) at the time of the Sodom and Gomorrah narrative, the Sodomites never consented to those laws. Moses got the consent of Abraham's people to be governed by the laws issued by God (Exodus 24.3, 24.7). The Sodomites were never asked, knew nothing about those laws, and had their own laws, customs and traditions and, most likely, their own gods. Thus, it could be said that the Sodomites were being held to laws that they did not consent to or even know about.

With sin being disobedience to God, and with the Sodomites not believing in God and not knowing or consenting to God's laws, the foundation for punishing the Sodomites is not clear, to say nothing of being unable to identify whether the "sin" was grounded in homosexuality, use of force, inhospitality or something else.

We can and do speculate about the purpose of the Sodom and Gomorrah narrative, but there is no speculation as to the meaning and purpose of the Gibeah narrative.

---

* We tend to lose sight of this. It is not sinful to run a red light. It is bad conduct, illegal conduct, but not sinful. Sin arises only in disobedience to what God wants and commands. Only the words of the Bible, the only divine source we have, tell us what God wants and commands. The Bible is God's Holy Book and God spoke only in that. If it's not in the Bible, there is no disobedience and thus no sin.

The Gibeah Narrative

A man with his concubine and his servant riding on donkeys were returning from Bethlehem in Judah to his home in the hill country of Ephraim. They turned aside on the way to spend the night in Gibeah, which belonged to tribe of Benjamin, and sat in the city's open square but nobody invited them to their home to spend the night (Judges 19.1-15). An old man also from the hill country of Ephraim and residing in Gibeah saw the wayfarers in the square, spoke with them and invited them into his home for the night and they ate and drank there (Judges 19.16-21).

"While they were enjoying themselves, the men of the city, a perverse lot, surrounded the house, and started pounding on the door. They said to the old man, the master of the house, 'Bring out the man who came into your house, so that we may have intercourse with him.' And the man, the master of the house, went out to them and said to them, 'No, my brothers, do not act so wickedly. Since this man is my guest, do not do this vile thing. Here are my virgin daughter and his concubine; let me bring them out now. Ravish them and do whatever you want to them; but against this man do not do such a vile thing.' " (Judges 19.22-24)

The men of Gibeah did not accept old man's offer and the visitor thereupon casts his concubine out to the men of Gibeah. They wantonly rape and abuse her through the night and let her go at dawn (Judges 19.25). In the morning she was found lying at the door of the house, presumably dead although that wasn't specifically stated. She did not answer when spoken to and the visitor put her on the donkey and set out for home (Judges 19.26-28). At home, he cut her into twelve pieces and sent them to the twelve tribes (Judges 19.29) asking them to take action against Gibeah. A tribal assembly considered what had happened and the city of Gibeah was condemned. The tribe of Benjamin supported Gibeah and war ensued between Benjamin and the other tribes with the Benjaminites almost getting wiped out.

The visitor cast his concubine out, apparently to save himself from being raped. He may have killed her as it was not stated that she was dead on the threshold when he found her. The motivations for his actions are not clear.

Still, the Gibeah narrative was the model for the priests who later wrote the Sodom and Gomorrah narrative and added it to the first Bible. The Gibeah narrative did have the same crucial elements of a visiting male guest being offered hospitality, of threatened multiple male rape by a body of local men, of an offer of a virgin daughter, and of plea based on hospitality.

God did not kill in the Gibeah narrative, which was the pattern in the first Bible as God was there portrayed as non-violent and never killing. God played no part in the Gibeah narrative, not even being mentioned. The men of Gibeah were called wicked and the proposed homosexual rape called vile, but there was no mention of the word "sin" or other indicia of the holiness theme the priests would later develop.

The rape was later called a criminal act and the concubine called a wife (Judges 20.3-4, 20.12) in priestly additions to the narrative. The first Bible's Gibeah narrative is told in terms of rape being a vile thing (Judges 19.24), not in criminal terms based on any existing law. At the time the Gibeah narrative was written and took place, the Mount Sinai narrative and the Ten Commandments and other laws of Moses hadn't yet been added by the priests to the first Bible. So, just like it was with respect to the Sodom and Gomorrah narrative having taken place in the time of Abraham, the priests hadn't yet added the laws of Moses to the first Bible. Thus, in both narratives, the Sodom and Gomorrah narrative and the Gibeah narrative, there were no laws in the Bible when the respective events took place.

This leads to another similarity in the two narratives. At the time of the Gibeah narrative, the communities that existed had a common heritage and it could be said that the traditions and customs of that society provide the rules the communities lived under. The Sodomites had a similar, earlier, community, but Abraham didn't.

THE MEANING AND PURPOSE OF THE GIBEAH NARRATIVE is clear on the face of the first Bible. At the time the Gibeah narrative was written, the Promised Land had been conquered (the first Bible's text as to this appears today in the Book of Joshua) and the land was ruled by a series of judges (today appearing in the Book of Judges, which follows the Book of Joshua).

Governance of the conquered land had not gone well and much of the original text in the Book of Judges reflected the rationale for the formation of a monarchy, the first monarch being King Saul (largely covered in the first Book of Samuel) and the second being King David (largely covered in the second Book of Samuel).

Much was made at the time the land was ruled by judges that there was then no king ruling the land (Judges 18.1, 19.1). The implication was that the people then did what they wanted, and a monarch would set them right. Specifically, it was the Gibeah narrative that triggered the intertribal fighting that ultimately led to the people demanding the formation of a monarchy to govern themselves (1 Samuel 8.4, 8.19-22). Thus, the story of Gibeah was of a community where everyone did what they wanted and ultimately showing that a king was needed to govern the land.

Thus, the purpose of the Gibeah narrative wasn't as narrow as criticizing homosexuality, use of force, or inhospitality but rather of a community requiring law and order enforced by a monarch so as to keep from running amuck. That was the simple purpose of the Gibeah narrative, portrayed without supernatural aspects, without angels, without raining of sulfur and fire or other violence of God. It was the people who fought and killed in the time Gibeah, not God.

The destruction of Gibeah would not have been in the way of God as God was portrayed in the first Bible.

Comparing the Two Narratives

A comparison of the two narratives, Sodom and Gomorrah & Gibeah, doesn't yield much because it largely follows the vastly different story patterns used by the priests in their additions and those of the author of the first Bible.

The first Bible largely portrayed a non-violent God who was content to stand by to help His people when they needed help, as in exiting Egypt, but otherwise not interfering in how the people lived their lives. God did not make any demands of His people, did not issue any laws to govern them and otherwise let the people do what they wanted subject only to their not overstepping the divine boundary by becoming too godly.

This is seen in the Gibeah narrative in that God played no role in it. The people did what they did with God not interfering. This non-violent God did not destroy the city of Gibeah and all the inhabitants in it. This God did not kill. This God did not sit in judgment, accepting His people as they were because He did not tell them to be otherwise. He issued no laws and didn't use the concept of "sin" to control what His people did. The word "sin" wasn't mentioned in the Gibeah narrative, not to mention the "grave" sin God sought to find in the priest's Sodom and Gomorrah narrative.

The message and meaning of the Gibeah narrative is most clear, while that of the Sodom and Gomorrah narrative is puzzling at best. The Gibeah narrative fits into the story of the people as presented in the first Bible and plays an important part in showing why the establishment of a monarchy became necessary to rule the land and keep the people in line.

As was the pattern in the first Bible, the Gibeah text is concise and no punches are pulled. There are no niceties to be obeyed, so the story is told as it was with all its warts. The rape does take place, a particularly brutal one leading to death. The visitor is starkly portrayed, contributing to his concubine's death if not being the final instrument. We are told what he did with his concubine's body, which was dreadful, and we can assume his motive was revenge against the men of Gibeah, but he is not castigated, labeled or otherwise explained. This is the way of the first Bible. Concise but with adequate detail to explain what happened without superfluous embellishments or explanations.

In stark contrast, the priestly additions to the first Bible, which additions included the Sodom and Gomorrah narrative, portray God differently. The priestly additions dominate today's Bible because they were so voluminous, relegating the original text of the first Bible to small segments here and there. Thus, the biblical text shifts back and forth from new to old and back again, creating conflicts, inconsistencies, and statements or events that do not make sense in the context presented. The most important differences in the old and new text were in the way God was portrayed, in the extent to which God intervened on earth, and in the emphasis on sin.

The God portrayed in the first Bible did not destroy Gibeah, while the God portrayed in the Sodom and Gomorrah narrative did destroy the two cities and others in the Plain. The God that destroyed Sodom was concerned with sin and insisted on some level of righteous conduct, not specifically defined but wrapped up in God's general condemnation of wickedness. This God drew distinctions between wickedness and righteousness without having then even defined these terms and without then having even told the people what He wanted since His commandments and other laws were made known much later.

This time dislocation, applying commandments and laws not yet promulgated, appears in the priestly text because the priests were making retroactive additions to a story already told in the first Bible.

Thus, there is a lack of inherent consistency in the story being told by the priests, while the first Bible had inherent consistency because it was written by a single author from passed-down oral transmissions that made sense to the people and withstood the test of time. The first Bible didn't have to deal with retroactive additions.

The priestly additions effectively apply laws that haven't yet been promulgated by God and apply standards to the Sodomites that were not known to that people. The time dislocation presented an insurmountable problem that appears to have led the priests to a forced vagueness since they couldn't or wouldn't be precise as to what the grave sin was. That is why we do not know what the Sodom and Gomorrah narrative means and stands for while we are very clear about the meaning and purpose of the Gibeah narrative.

The Fifth Rationale for Sodom's Destruction

A fifth rationale for Sodom's destruction arises from another aspect underlying the priestly additions to the first Bible. At the time the priests were making their retroactive additions to the first Bible, their purpose and goal was to transform[*] the religion from one revolving around the land (the Promised Land) to one revolving around the laws they were about to insert into the first Bible (the so-called laws of Moses). Continued ownership of the land had proven unreliable with the sacking of Jerusalem by the Egyptians, the conquest of the Northern areas by the Assyrians and the conquest of the rest of the Promised Land by the Babylonians and the exile in Babylon.

The priests inserted God's commandments, laws and ordinances into the first Bible and commenced on a program to get

---

[*] This is covered in detail in the author's book *"Biblical Verses, A Frank Study of the Old Testament and Hebrew Bible."*

the people to comply with them. To do that, the priests started to portray a fearsome God so as to instill the fear of God in the people so that the people would obey the new laws. This is where the portrayal of a stern, unrelenting and largely uncompassionate and violent God came from. The priests couldn't continue portraying the forgiving and compassionate God of the first Bible and yet expect compliance with their new laws.

This explains the total destruction of entire communities, specifically Sodom and Gomorrah, without any attempt to spare innocent women and children obviously inhabiting those communities. More of this indiscriminate killing by God is to be found in other priestly additions to the first Bible, like God spreading necessarily indiscriminate plagues or casting poisonous snakes against his own people (Numbers 21.6). The priests used these narratives and many more like them to instill in the people the fear of this very fearsome God pursuant to their righteous purpose of transforming the religion. The priests weren't being mean about it. Portraying a fearsome God helped them mold the society they thought best for their people.

Thus, in addition to the previously mentioned four rationales for the destruction of Sodom (homosexuality, use of force, inhospitality and the community running amuck), perhaps a fifth rationale should be added: the introduction of a fearsome God.

Appendix

The Full Text of the First Bible

The italicized headings inserted below are not part of the first Bible. The headings are included to identify which book of today's Old Testament / Hebrew Bible the first Bible's text was extracted from, and also to assist scanning by readers.

The verse numbers are the same as in today's Bible, with omitted words or phrases indicated by the use of three dots ("..."), and four dots used if the omitted words or phrase occurs at the end of a sentence. Otherwise, four dots signify omitted sentences or paragraphs. A gap in verse numbers indicates omitted verses, verses that are in today's Bible but did not appear in the first Bible.

The English translation is that of the New Revised Standard Version of The New Oxford Annotated Bible, Third Edition.

Extracted From the Book of Genesis

Creation

2.4 …. In the day that the LORD God made the earth and the heavens, **2.5** when no plant of the field was yet in the earth and no herb of the field had yet sprung up – for the LORD God had not caused it to rain upon the earth, and there was no one to till the ground … – **2.7** then the LORD God formed man from the dust of the ground, and breathed into his nostrils the breath of life; and the man became a living being. **2.8** And the LORD God planted a garden in Eden, in the east; and there he put the man whom he had formed. **2.9** Out of the ground the LORD God made to grow every tree that is pleasant to the sight and good for food, the tree of life also in the midst of the garden, and the tree of the knowledge of good and evil.

2.15 The LORD God took the man and put him in the Garden of Eden to till it and keep it. **2.16** And the LORD God commanded the man, "You may freely eat of every tree of the garden; **2.17** but of the tree of the knowledge of good and evil you shall not eat, for in the day that you eat of it you shall die."

2.18 Then the LORD God said, " … I will make him a helper …." **2.19** So out of the ground the LORD God formed every animal of the field …. **2.20** … but for the man there was not found a helper …. **2.21** So the LORD God caused a deep sleep to fall upon the man, and he slept; then he took one of his ribs and closed up its place …. **2.22** And the rib that the LORD God had taken from the man he made into a woman ….

Genesis (Cont'd)

Garden of Eden

3.1 Now the serpent was more crafty than any other wild animal that the LORD God had made. He said to the woman, "Did God say, 'You shall not eat from any tree in the garden'?" **3.2** The woman said to the serpent, "We may eat of the fruit of the trees in the garden; **3.3** but God said, 'You shall not eat of the fruit of the tree that is in the middle of the garden, ... or you shall die.' " **3.4** But the serpent said to the woman, "You will not die; **3.5** for God knows that when you eat of it your eyes will be opened, and you will be like God, knowing good and evil." **3.6** So when the woman saw that the tree was good for food, and that is was a delight to the eyes, and that the tree was to be desired to make one wise, she took of its fruit and ate; and ... he ate. **3.7** Then the eyes of both were opened ....

3.8 They heard the sound of the LORD God walking in the garden at the time of the evening breeze, and the man ... hid ... from the presence of the LORD God among the trees of the garden. **3.9** But the LORD God called to the man, and said to him, "Where are you?" **3.10** He said, "I heard the sound of you in the garden, and I was afraid, because I was naked; and I hid myself." **3.11** He said, "Who told you that you were naked? Have you eaten from the tree of which I commanded you not to cat?" **3.12** The man said, "The woman ... gave me fruit from the tree, and I ate" **3.13** Then the LORD God said to the woman, "What is this that you have done?" The woman said, "The serpent tricked me, and I ate." **3.21** And the LORD God made garments of skins ... and clothed them.

3.22 Then the LORD God said, "See the man has become like one of us, knowing good and evil; and now, he might reach out his hand and take also from the tree of life, and eat, and live forever ...." **3.24** He drove out the man; and at the east of the garden of Eden he placed the cherubim, and a sword flaming and turning to guard the way to the tree of life.

4.1 Now the man knew his wife ..., and she conceived ....**6.1** When people began to multiply on the face of the ground, and daughters were born to them, **6.2** the sons ... saw that they were fair; and they took wives for themselves of all that they chose.

Tower of Babel

11.2 ... [A]s they migrated from the east, they came upon a plain in the land of Shinar and settled there. **11.3** And they said to one another, ... **11.4** ..."Come, let us build ourselves a city, and a tower with its top in the heavens, and let us make a name for ourselves ...." **11.5** The LORD came down to see the city and the tower.... **11.6** And the LORD said, "Look, they are one people, and they have all one language; and this is only the beginning of what they will do; nothing that they propose to do will be impossible for them. **11.7** Come, let us go down, and confuse their language there, so that they will not understand one another's speech." **11.8** So ... they left off building the city... **11.9** ... called Babel ....

Abraham

12.1 Now the LORD said to Abraham, "Go from your country and your kindred and your father's house to the land that I will show you. **12.2** I will make of you a great nation, ... and make your name great ...." **12.4** So Abraham went, as the LORD had told him; and .... **12.5** ... took his wife Sarah ... and all the possessions ... they had acquired in Haran .... When they had come to the land of Canaan, **12.6** Abraham passed through the land to the place at Shechem, to the oak of Moreh. At that time the Canaanites were in the land. **12.7** Then the LORD appeared to Abraham and said, "To your offspring I will give this land." .... **12.8** From there he moved on to the hill country on the east of Bethel .... **12.9** And Abraham journeyed on by stages toward the Negeb.

12.10 Now there was a famine in the land. So Abraham went down to Egypt to reside there as an alien .... **12.11** When he was about to enter Egypt, he said to his wife Sarah, "I know well that you are a woman beautiful in appearance; **12.12** and when the Egyptians see you, they will say, 'This is his wife'; then they will kill me, but they will let you live. **12.13** Say you are my sister, so that it may go well with me because of you, and that my life may be spared on your account." **12.14** When Abraham entered Egypt the Egyptians saw that the woman was very beautiful. **12.15** When the officials of Pharaoh saw her, they praised her to Pharaoh. And the woman was taken into Pharaoh's house. **12.16** And for her sake he dealt well with Abraham; and he had sheep, oxen, male donkeys, male and female slaves, female donkeys, and camels. **12.17** But the LORD afflicted Pharaoh and his house with ... plagues because of Sarah .... **12.18** So Pharaoh called Abraham and said, "What is this you have done to me? Why did you not tell me that she was your wife? **12.19** Why did you say, 'She is my sister,' so that I took her for my wife? Now then, here is your wife, take her, and be gone." **12.20** And Pharaoh gave his men orders concerning him; and they set him on the way, with his wife and all that he had. **13.1** So Abraham went up from Egypt, he and his wife, and all that he had ... with him, into the Negeb. **13.2** Now Abraham was very rich in livestock, in silver and in gold.

13.3 He journeyed on by stages from the Negeb as far as Bethel, to the place where his tent had been at the beginning .... **18.1** The LORD appeared to Abraham by the oaks of Mamre, as he sat at the entrance of his tent in the heat of the day. **18.2** He looked up and saw three men standing near him. **18.3** He said, "…. **18.5** Let me bring you bring a little bread, that you may refresh yourselves …." **18.8** Then he took curds and milk and the calf that he had prepared, and set it before them; and he stood by them under the tree while they ate. **18.10** Then one said, "I will surely return to you in due season, and your wife Sarah shall have a son." **21.1** The LORD dealt with Sarah as he had said …. **21.2** Sarah conceived and bore Abraham a son …. **21.3** Abraham gave the name Isaac to his son ….

Isaac

24.1 Now Abraham was old, well advanced in years. **24.2** Abraham said to his servant … " …. **24.4** … [G]o to my country and to my kindred and get a wife for my son Isaac." **24.10** Then the servant took ten of his master's camels and departed, taking all kinds of choice gifts from his master; and he set out ….

24.63 Isaac went out in the evening to walk in the field; and looking up, he saw camels coming. **24.64** And Rebekah looked up, and when she saw Isaac, she slipped quickly from the camel, **24.65** and said to the servant, "Who is the man over there, walking in the field to meet us?" The servant said, "It is my master." So she took her veil and covered herself. **24.66** And the servant told Isaac all the things that he had done. **24.67** Then Isaac brought her into his mother Sarah's tent. He took Rebekah, and she became his wife; and he loved her. So Isaac was comforted after his mother's death. **25.8** Abraham breathed his last and died in a good old age.

Genesis (Cont'd)

Jacob

25.21 Isaac prayed to the LORD for his wife, because she was barren; and the LORD granted his prayer, and his wife Rebekah conceived. **25.24** When her time to give birth was at hand, there were twins in her womb. **25.27** When the boys grew up, Esau was a skillful hunter, a man of the field, while Jacob was a quiet man, living in tents. **25.28** Isaac loved Esau, because he was fond of game, but Rebekah loved Jacob.

25.29 Once when Jacob was cooking a stew, Esau came in from the field, and .... **25.30** ... said to Jacob, "Let me eat some of that red stuff, for I am famished!" **25.31** Jacob said, "First sell me your birthright." **25.33** ... So he ... sold his birthright to Jacob. **25.34** Then Jacob gave Esau bread and lentil stew, and he ate and drank, and rose and went his way....

27.5 Now Rebekah was listening when Isaac spoke to his son Esau. **27.6** Rebekah said to her son Jacob, "I heard your father say to your brother Esau, **27.7** 'Bring me game, and prepare for me savory food to eat, that I may bless you before the LORD before I die.' **27.8** Now therefore, my son, obey my word as I command you. **27.9** Go to the flock, and get me two choice kids, so that I may prepare from them savory food for your father, such as he likes; **27.10** and you shall take it to your father to eat, so that he may bless you before he dies." **27.14** So he went and got them and brought them to his mother; and his mother prepared savory food, such as his father loved. **27.17** Then she handed the savory food ... to her son Jacob.

27.18 So he went in to his father, and said, "My father"; and he said, "Here I am; who are you, my son?" **27.19** Jacob said to his father, "I am Esau your firstborn. I have done as you told me; now sit up and eat of my game, so that you may bless me." **27.24** He said, "Are you really my son Esau?" He answered, "I am." **27.25** Then he said, "Bring it to me ...." So he brought it to him, and he ate; and he .... **27.27** ... blessed him ....

27.30 As soon as Isaac had finished blessing Jacob, when Jacob had scarcely gone out from the presence of his father Isaac, his brother Esau came in from his hunting. **27.31** He also prepared savory food, and brought it to his father .... **27.33** Then Isaac trembled violently, and said, "Who was it then that hunted game and brought it to me, and I ate it all before you came, and I have blessed him? ---yes, and blessed he shall be!" **27.34** When Esau heard his father's words, he cried out with an exceedingly great and bitter cry, and said to his father, "Bless me, me also, father!" **27.37** Isaac answered Esau, "I have already made him your lord, and I have given him all his brothers as servants .... What then can I do for you, my son?"

27.41 Now Esau hated Jacob ... and Esau said ... , "The days of mourning for my father are approaching; then I will kill my brother Jacob." **27.42** But the words of ... Esau were told to Rebekah; so she ... called ... Jacob and said to him, " .... **27.43** Now... flee at once to my brother Laban in Haran, **27.44** and stay with him ... until your brother's fury turns .... **27.45** away, and he forgets what you have done to him ....

29.13 When Laban heard the news about his sister's son Jacob, he ran to meet him; he embraced and kissed him, and brought him to this house. Jacob .... **29.14** ...stayed with him a month. **29.16** Now Laban had two daughters; the name of the elder was Leah, and the name of the younger was Rachel. **29.18** Jacob loved Rachel; so he said, "I will serve you seven years for your younger daughter

Rachel." **29.20** So Jacob served seven years for Rachel, and they seemed to him but a few days because of the love he had for her.

29.21 Then Jacob said to Laban, "Give me my wife that I may go in to her, for my time is completed." **29.22** So Laban gathered together all the people of the place, and made a feast. **29.23** But in the evening he took his daughter Leah and brought her to Jacob; and he went into her. **29.25** When morning came, it was Leah! And Jacob said to Laban, "What is this you have done to me? Did I not serve with you for Rachel? Why then have you deceived me?" **29.26** Laban said, "This is not done in our country – giving the younger before the firstborn. **29.27** Complete the week of this one, and we will give you the other also in return for serving me another seven years." **29.28** Jacob did so, and completed her week; then Laban gave him his daughter Rachel as a wife. **29.30** So Jacob went in to Rachel also, and he loved Rachel more than Leah. He served Laban for another seven years. **29.31** When the LORD saw that Leah was unloved, he opened her womb; but Rachel was barren. **30.22** Then God remembered Rachel, … and opened her womb.

31.1 Now Jacob heard that the sons of Laban were saying, "Jacob has taken all that was our father's; he has gained all this wealth from what belonged to our father." **31.2** And Jacob saw that Laban did not regard him as favorably as he did before. **31.17** So Jacob arose, and set his children and his wives on camels.

32.3 Jacob sent messengers before him to his brother Esau …. **32.6** The messengers returned to Jacob saying, "We came to your brother Esau, and he is coming to meet you, and four hundred men are with him." **33.1** Now Jacob looked up and saw Esau coming, and four hundred men with him. So he …. **33.3** … went … bowing himself to the ground seven times, until he came near his brother.

33.4 But Esau ran to meet him, and embraced him, and fell on his neck and kissed him, and they wept.

35. 16 Then ...Rachel was in childbirth, and she had hard labor. **35.18** ... [H]is father called him Benjamin. **35.19** So Rachel died, and she was buried .... **35.22** .... Now the sons of Jacob were twelve. **35.23** The sons of Leah: Reuben ..., Simeon, Levi, Judah, Issachar, and Zebulun. **35.24** The sons of Rachel: Joseph and Benjamin. **35.25** The sons of Bilhah, Rachel's maid: Dan and Naphtali. **35.26** The sons of Zilpah, Leah's maid: Gad and Asher.

35.27 Jacob came to his father Isaac at Mamre .... **35.29** And Isaac breathed his last; he died and was gathered to his people, old and full of days; and his sons Esau and Jacob buried him.

Joseph

37.1 Jacob settled in the land where his father had lived as an alien, the land of Canaan. **37.5** Once Joseph had a dream, and when he told it to his brothers, they hated him .... **37.6** He said to them, "Listen to this dream that I dreamed. **37.7** There we were, binding sheaves in the field. Suddenly my sheaf rose and stood upright; then your sheaves gathered around it, and bowed down to my sheaf."

37.12 Now his brothers went to pasture their father's flock .... **37.19** They said to one another, "Here comes this dreamer. **37.20** Come now, let us kill him and throw him into one of the pits; then we shall say that a wild animal has devoured him, and we shall see what will become his dreams. **37.23** So when Joseph came to his brothers, they stripped him of his robe, the long robe with sleeves that he wore; **37.24** and they ... threw him into a pit. **37.25** Then they sat down to eat; and looking up they saw a caravan ... on their

Genesis (Cont'd)

way … to Egypt. **37.26** Then Judah said to his brothers, "What profit is it if we kill our brother and conceal his blood? **37.27** Come, let us sell him … and not lay our hands on him, for his is our brother …." And his brothers agreed …. **37.28** When some Midianite traders passed by, they… sold him …. And they took Joseph to Egypt.

37.31 Then they took Joseph's robe, slaughtered a goat, and dipped the robe in the blood. **37.32** They had the long robe with sleeves taken to their father, and they said, "This we have found; see now whether it is your son's robe or not." **37.33** He recognized it, and said, "It is my son's robe! A wild animal has devoured him; Joseph is without doubt torn to pieces." **37.34** Then Jacob tore his garments, and put sackcloth on his loins, and mourned for his son many days.

41.14 … Pharaoh sent for Joseph …. **41.15** And Pharaoh said to Joseph, "I have had a dream, and there is no one who can interpret it. I have heard it said of you that when you hear a dream you can interpret it." **41.17** Then Pharaoh …. **41.24** … told it …. **41.25** Then Joseph said to Pharaoh, "…. **41.29** There will come seven years of great plenty throughout all the land of Egypt. **41.30** After them there will be arise seven years of famine …. **41.34** Let Pharaoh proceed to appoint overseers over the land, and take one-fifth of the produce of the land of Egypt during the seven plenteous years. **41.36** That food shall be a reserve for the land against the seven years of famine …." **41.55** … Pharaoh said to all the Egyptians, "Go to Joseph; what he says to you, do."

42.1 … Jacob … said to his sons, …. **42.2** "I have heard … that there is grain in Egypt; go down and buy grain for us there, that we may live and not die." **45.1** Then Joseph could no longer control himself before all those who stood by him, and he cried out, "Send everyone away from me." So no one stayed with him when Joseph made himself known to his brothers. **45.2** And he wept so loudly that the Egyptians heard it, and the household of the Pharaoh heard it. **45.16** When the report was heard in Pharaoh's house, ... Pharaoh and his servants were pleased. **45.17** Pharaoh said to Joseph, "Say to your brothers 'Do this: ... go back to the land of Canaan. **45.18** Take your father and your households and come to me, so that I may give you the best of the land of Egypt ....'"

47.1 So Joseph went and told Pharaoh, "My father and my brothers, with their flocks and herds and all that they possess have come from the land of Canaan; they are now in the land of Goshen." **47.5** Then Pharaoh said to Joseph, ".... **47.6** The land of Egypt is before you; settle your father and your brothers in the best part of the land; let them live in the land of Goshen; and if you know that there are capable men among them, put them in charge of my livestock."

49.33 When Jacob ended his charge to his sons, he drew up his feet into the bed, breathed his last, and was gathered to his people. **50.22** So Joseph remained in Egypt, he and his father's household ....

Extracted From the Book of Exodus

Moses

1.6 Then Joseph died, and all his brothers, and that whole generation. **2.1** Now a man from the house of Levi went and married a Levite woman. **2.2** The woman conceived and bore a son; and …. **2.10** … she … named him Moses ….

2.15 … Moses … settled in the land of Midian, and sat down by a well. **2.16** The priest of Midian had seven daughters. They came to draw water, and filled the troughs to water their father's flock. **2.17** But some shepherds came and drove them away. Moses got up and came to their defense and watered their flock. **2.18** When they returned to their father Reuel, he said "How is it that you have come back so soon today?" **2.19** They said, "An Egyptian helped us against the shepherds; he even drew water for us and watered the flock." **2.20** He said to his daughters, "Where is he? Why did you leave the man? Invite him to break bread." **2.21** Moses agreed to stay with the man, and he gave Moses his daughter Zipporah in marriage. **2.22** She bore a son, and he named him Gershom ….

Exiting Egypt

4.18 Moses went back to this father-in-law … and said to him, "Please let me go back to my kindred in Egypt and see whether they are still living." **4.19** "The LORD said to Moses…, 'Go back to Egypt…'" **4.20** So Moses took his wife and his sons, and … went back to the land of Egypt …. **4.21** And the LORD said to Moses, "When you go back to Egypt, …. **4.22** you shall say to Pharaoh, …. **5.1** 'Let my people go ….'" **5.2** But the Pharaoh said, "…. I do not know the LORD, and I will not let Israel go."

12.37 The Israelites journeyed from Ramses to Succoth .... **12.38** A mixed crowd also went up with them, and livestock in great numbers, both flocks and herds. **12.39** They baked unleavened cakes of the dough that they had brought out of Egypt .... **13.21** The LORD went in front of them in a pillar of cloud by day, to lead them along the way, and in a pillar of fire by night, to give them light, so that they might travel by day and by night. **13.22** Neither the pillar of cloud by day nor the pillar of fire by night left its place in front of the people.

14.5 When the king of Egypt was told that the people had fled, ... **14.6** ... he had his chariot made ready, and took his army with him. **14.9** The Egyptians pursued them ...; they overtook them camped by the sea .... **14.21** .... The LORD drove the sea back by a strong east wind all night, and turned the sea into dry land .... **14.22** The Israelites went into the sea on dry ground .... **14.23** The Egyptians pursued, and went into the sea after them .... **14.24** At the morning watch the LORD ... threw the Egyptian army into panic. **14.25** ... The Egyptians said, "Let us flee from the Israelites, for the LORD is fighting for them against Egypt."

In The Wilderness

15.22 Then Moses ordered Israel to set out from the Red Sea, and they went into the wilderness of Shur. **16.4** ... [T]he LORD said to Moses, "I am going to rain bread from heaven for you, and each day the people shall go out and gather enough for that day .... **16.31** ... Israel called it manna .... **16.35** The Israelites ate manna ... until they came to the border of the land of Canaan.

Extracted From the Book of Leviticus

No first Bible text is found in Leviticus.

Extracted From the Book of Numbers

In The Wilderness (Cont'd)

13.17 Moses sent ... to spy out the land of Canaan, and said ... , "Go up there into the Negeb, and go up into the hill country, **13.18** and see what the land is like ....". **13.27** And they told him, "We came to the land to which you sent us; it flows with milk and honey, and this is its fruit. **13.28** Yet the people who live in the land are strong, and the towns are fortified and very large .... **13.31** We are not able to go up against this people, for they are stronger than we."

20.1 The Israelites, the whole congregation, came into the wilderness of Zin in the first month, and the people stayed in Kadesh ....**20.14** Moses sent messengers from Kadesh to the King of Edom, "Thus says your brother Israel; .... **20.17** let us pass through your land. We will not pass through the field or vineyard, or drink water from any well; we will go along the King's Highway, not turning aside to the right hand or to the left until we have passed through your territory." **20.20** But he said, "You shall not pass through." And Edom came out against them with a large force, heavily armed. **20.21** Thus Edom refused to give Israel passage through their territory; so Israel turned away from them.

21.21 Then Israel sent messengers to King Sihon of the Amorites, saying, **21.22** "Let me pass through your land; we will not turn aside into field or vineyard; we will not drink the water of any well; we will go by the King's Highway until we have passed through your territory." **21.23** But Sihon would not allow Israel to pass through his territory. Sihon gathered all his people together, and ... fought against Israel. **21.24** Israel put him to the sword and took possession of his land .... **21.32** Moses sent to spy out Jazer; and they captured its villages and dispossessed the Amorites who were there. **21.33** Then they turned and went up the road to Bashan; and King Og of Bashan came out against them .... **21.35** So they killed him ... and they took possession of his land. **22.1** The Israelites set out, and camped in the plains of Moab across the Jordan from Jericho.

Extracted From the Book of Deuteronomy

In The Wilderness (Cont'd)

34.5 Then Moses ... died there in the land of Moab .... **34.6** He was buried in a valley in the land of Moab ....

The Five Book Torah Would End Here

Extracted From the Book of Joshua

Conquering the Promised Land

2.1 Then Joshua son of Nun sent two men secretly ... as spies, saying, "Go view the land, especially Jericho." **2.22** They departed and went into the country and stayed there three days .... **2.23** Then the two men came down again from the hill country. They crossed over, came to Joshua ..., and told him all that had happened to them.

Joshua (Cont'd)

4.19 The people came up out of the Jordan … and they camped in Gilgal on the east border of Jericho. **5.12** The manna ceased on the day they ate the produce of the land ….**6.1** Now Jericho was shut up inside and out because of the Israelites …. **6.10** To the people Joshua gave this command: "You shall not shout or let your voice be heard, nor shall you utter a word, until … I tell you to shout. Then you shall shout." **6.15** On the … day they rose early, at dawn, and marched around the city seven times. **6.16** And … Joshua said to the people, "Shout! …." **6.20** So the people shouted, and the trumpets were blown …., and the wall fell down flat; so the people charged straight ahead into the city and captured it.

11.23 So Joshua took the … land, … and Joshua gave it for an inheritance to Israel according to their tribal allotments. And the land had rest from war. **13.1** Now Joshua was old and advanced in years; and …. **24.29** … Joshua … died ….

Extracted From the Book of Judges

Abimelech

9.1 Now Abimelech son of Jerubbaal went to Shechem to his mother's kinfolk and said to them and to the whole clan of his mother's family, **9.2** "Say in the hearing of all the lords of Shechem, 'Which is better for you, that all seventy of the sons of Jerubbaal rule over you, or that one rule over you?' …. " **9.3** So his mother's kinsfolk spoke all these words on his behalf in the hearing of all the lords of Shechem; and their hearts inclined to follow Abimelech, for they said, "He is our brother." **9.4** They gave him seventy pieces of silver … with which Abimelech hired worthless and reckless fellows, who followed him. **9.5** He went to his father's house at

Judges (Cont'd)

Ophrah, and killed his brothers …, seventy men, on one stone …. **9.6** Then all the lords of Shechem … made Abimelech king …. **9.22** Abimelech ruled … three years.

9.26 When Gaal son of Ebed moved into Shechem with his kinsfolk, the lords of Shechem put confidence in him. **9.28** Gaal … said, "Who is Abimelech, and who are we of Shechem, that we should serve him? …. **9.39** So Gaal went out at the head of the lords of Shechem, and fought with Abimelech. **9.40** Abimelech chased him, and he fled before him. **9.50** Then Abimelech went to Thebez, and encamped against Thebez, and took it. **9.51** But there was a strong tower within the city, and all the men and women and all the lords of the city fled to it and shut themselves in; and they went to the roof of the tower. **9.52** Abimelech came to the tower, and fought against it, and came near to the entrance of the tower to burn it with fire. **9.53** But a certain woman threw an upper millstone on Abimelech's head, and crushed his skull …. **9.54** …. and he died.

Samson

14.1 Once Samson … **14.2** told his father and mother, "I saw a Philistine woman at Timnah; now get …. **14.3** … her for me, because she pleases me." **14.5** Then Samson went down with his father and mother to Timnah. When he came to the vineyards of Timnah, suddenly a young lion roared at ….**14.6** … him, and he tore the lion apart barehanded as one might tear apart a kid. **14.8** After a while he returned to marry her …. and he …. **14.10** … made a feast there as the young men were accustomed to do. **14.11** When the people saw him, they brought thirty companions to be with him. **14.19** …. In hot anger he went back to his father's house. **14.20** And Samson's wife was given to his companion, who had been his best man.

Judges (Cont'd)

15.1 After a while, … Samson went to visit his wife, bringing along a kid. He said "I want to go into my wife's room." …. **15.2** Her father said, "I was sure that you had rejected her; so I gave her to your companion …." **15.4** So Samson went and caught … foxes, and took some torches; and he turned the foxes tail to tail, and put a torch between each pair of tails. **15.5** When he had set fire to the torches, he let the foxes go into the standing grain of the Philistines, and burned up the shocks and the standing grain, as well as the vineyards and olive groves.

15.6 Then the Philistines asked, "Who has done this?" And they said, "Samson, son-in-law of the Timnite, because he has taken Samson's wife and given her to his companion." So the Philistines came up and burned her and her father. **15.7** Samson said to them, "If this is what you do, I swear that I will not stop until I have taken revenge on you." **15.8** He struck them down hip and thigh ….

16.1 Once Samson went to Gaza, where he saw a prostitute and went into her. **16.4** After this he fell in love with a woman in the valley of Sorek whose name was Delilah. **16.5** The lords of the Philistines came to her and said to her, "Coax him, and find out what makes his strength so great, and how we might overpower him, so that we may bind him in order to subdue him; and we each will give you … pieces of silver."

16.6 So Delilah said to Samson, "Please tell me what makes your strength so great, and how you could be bound, so that one could subdue you." **16.7** Samson said to her, "If they bind me with seven fresh bowstrings that are not dried out, then I shall be weak, and be like anyone else." **16.8** Then the lords of the Philistines brought her seven fresh bowstrings that had not dried out, and she bound him with them. **16.9** While men were lying in wait in an inner chamber, she said to him, "The Philistines are upon you, Samson!" But he snapped the bowstrings, as a strand of fiber snaps when it touches the fire ....

16.15 Then she said to him, "How can you say, 'I love you' when your heart is not with me? You have mocked me three times now and have not told me what makes your strength so great." **16.16** Finally, after she had nagged him with her words day after day, and pestered him, he was tired to death. **16.17** So he told her his whole secret, and said to her, " .... If my head were shaved, then my strength would leave me; I would become weak, and be like anyone else."

16.18 When Delilah realized that he had told her his whole secret, she sent and called the lords of the Philistines, saying, "This time come up, for he has told his whole secret to me." Then the lords of the Philistines came up to her, and brought the money in their hands. **16.19** She let him fall asleep on her lap; and she called a man, and had him shave off the seven locks of his head. He began to weaken, and his strength left him. **16.20** Then she said, "The Philistines are upon you, Samson!" When he awoke from his sleep, he thought, "I will go out as at other times, and shake myself free." **16.21** So the Philistines seized him and gouged out his eyes. They brought him down to Gaza and bound him with bronze shackles; and he ground at the mill in the prison. **16.22** But the hair on his head began to grow again after it had been shaved.

16.23 Now the lords of the Philistines gathered ... to rejoice .... **16.25** And when their hearts were merry, they said, "Call Samson, and let him entertain us." So they called Samson out of the prison, and he performed for them. They made him stand between the pillars; **16.26** and Samson said to the attendant who held him by the

Judges (Cont'd)

hand, "Let me feel the pillars on which the house rests, so that I may lean against them." **16.27** Now the house was full of men and women; all the lords of the Philistines were there, and on the roof there were … men and women, who looked on while Samson performed.

16.29 And Samson grasped the two middle pillars on which the house rested, and he leaned his weight against them, his right hand on the one and his left hand on the other. **16.30** Then Samson said, "Let me die with the Philistines." He strained with all his might; and the house fell on the lords and all the people who were in it ….

Micah

17.1 There was a man in the hill country of Ephraim whose name was Micah. **17.4** … [H]is mother took … pieces of silver, and gave it to the silversmith, who made it into an idol of cast metal; and it was in the house of Micah. **17.5** This man Micah had a shrine, and he made an ephod and teraphim, and installed one of his sons, who became his priest.

18.1 In those days there was no king in Israel. And in those days the tribe of the Danites was seeking for itself a territory to live in; for until then no territory among the tribes of Israel had been allotted to them. **18.2** So the Danites sent five valiant men … to spy out the land and to explore it …. When they came to the hill country of Ephraim, to the house of Micah, they stayed there. **18.7** The five men went on, and when they came to Laish, they observed the people who were there living securely …. **18.8** When they came their kinsfolk … , they said to them, …. **18.9** … "Come, let us go up against them; for we have seen the land, and it is very good …."

18.11 Six hundred men of the Danite clan, armed with weapons of war, set out … and went up and …. **18.13** … came to the house of Micah. **18.16** While the six hundred men … stood by the entrance to the gate, **18.17** the five men who had gone to spy out the land proceeded to enter and take the idol of cast metal, the ephod, and the teraphim. The priest was standing by the entrance to the gate with the six hundred men … **18.19** They said to him, "Keep quiet! Put your hand over your mouth, and come with us, and be to us … a priest. Is it better for you to be priest to the house of one person, or to be priest to a tribe and clan of Israel?" **18.20** Then the priest accepted the offer. He took the ephod, the teraphim, and the idol, and went along with the people. **18.21** So they resumed their journey ….

18.22 When they were some distance from the home of Micah, the men who were in the houses near Micah's house were called out, and they overtook the Danites. **18.23** They shouted to the Danites, who turned around and said to Micah, "What is the matter that you come with such a company?" **18.24** He replied, "You take my gods that I made, and the priest, and go away, and what have I left? How can you ask me, 'What is the matter?'" **18.25** And the Danites said to him, "You had better not let your voice be heard among us or else the hot-tempered fellows will attack you, and you will lose your life and the lives of your household." **18.26** Then the Danites went their way. When Micah saw that they were too strong for him, he turned and went back to his home.

18.27 The Danites, having taken what Micah had made, and the priest who belonged to him, came to Laish … and burned down the city. **18.28** …. They rebuilt the city, and lived in it. **18.29** They named the city Dan …. **18.30** Then the Danites set up the idol for themselves ….**18.31** So they maintained as their own Micah's idol ….

Judges (Cont'd)

Gibeah

19.1 In those days, when there was no king in Israel, a certain Levite residing in the remote parts of the hill country of Ephraim, took to himself a concubine from Bethlehem in Judah. **19.2** But his concubine became angry with him, and she went away from him to her father's house in Bethlehem and was there some four months. **19.3** Then her husband set out after her, to speak tenderly to her and bring her back …. **19.4** When he reached her father's house, the girl's father saw him and came with joy to meet him. **19.6** So the two men sat and ate and drank together, and the girl's father said to the man, "Why not spend the night and enjoy yourself?" **19.10** But the man would not spend the night; he got up and departed …. He had with him a couple of saddled donkeys, and his concubine with him …. **19.14** … and the sun went down on them near Gibeah, which belongs to Benjamin.

19.15 They turned aside there, …. went in and sat down in the open square of the city, but no one took them in to spend the night. **19.16** Then at evening there was an old man coming from his work in the field …. **19.17** When the old man looked up and saw the wayfarer in the open square of the city, he said, …. **19.20** "Peace be to you. I will care for all your wants; only do not spend the night in the square." **19.21** So he brought him to his house, and fed the donkeys; they washed their feet, and ate and drank.

19.22 While they were enjoying themselves, the men of the city, a perverse lot, surrounded the house, and started pounding on the door. They said to the old man, the master of the house, "Bring out the man who came into your house, so that we may have intercourse with him." **19.23** And the man … said to them, "No, my brothers, …. this man is my guest, do not do this vile thing. **19.24** Here are my virgin daughter and his concubine; let me bring them out now. Ravish them and do whatever you want to them ...." **19.25** But the men would not listen to him. So the man seized his concubine, and put her out to them. They wantonly raped her, and abused her all through the night until the morning. And as the dawn began to break, they let her go. **19.26** As morning appeared, the woman came and fell down at the door of the man's house where her master was, until it was light.

19.27 In the morning her master got up, opened the doors of the house, and when he went out to go on his way, there was his concubine lying at the door of the house with her hands on the threshold. **19.28** "Get up," he said to her, "we are going." But there was no answer. Then he put her on the donkey; and the man set out for his home.

19.29 When he had entered his house, he took a knife, and grasping his concubine he cut her into twelve pieces, limb by limb and sent her throughout all the territory of Israel. **19.30** Then he commanded the men whom he sent, saying "Thus shall you say to all the Israelites, 'Has such a thing ever happened ...? Consider it, take counsel, and speak out.'"

20.1 Then all the Israelites came out ... and ... assembled ... at Mizpah. **20.12** The tribes of Israel sent men through all the tribe of Benjamin, saying, "What crime is this that has been committed among you? **20.13** Now then, hand over those scoundrels in Gibeah, so that we may put them to death ...." But the Benjaminites would not listen .... **20.14** The Benjaminites came together out of the towns to Gibeah, to go out to battle against the Israelites. **20.34** There came against Gibeah ... picked men out of all Israel, and the battle was fierce.... **20.36** Then the Benjaminites saw that they were defeated.

Extracted From the Book of Ruth

No first Bible text is found in Ruth.

Extracted From the Book of 1 Samuel

Samuel

1.2 .... Hannah had no children. **1.10** She was deeply distressed ... and wept bitterly. **1.11** She made this vow, "O LORD ..., if only you ... give to your servant a male child, I will set him before you as a nazirite and ... no razor shall touch his head." **1.20** In due time, Hannah conceived and bore a son. She named him Samuel .... **1.24** When she had weaned him, she ... brought him to the house of the LORD at Shiloh; and ....**1.28** .... left him there .... **2. 21** .... And the boy Samuel grew up in the presence of the LORD.

7.15 Samuel judged Israel all the days of his life. **8.1** When Samuel became old, he made his sons judges over Israel. **8.19** But the people refused to listen to the voice of Samuel; they said, "No! but we are determined to have a king over us ...."

10.20 Then Samuel brought all the tribes of Israel near, and the tribe of Benjamin was taken by lot. **10.21** He brought the tribe of Benjamin near by its families, and the family of the Matrites was taken by lot. Finally he brought the family of the Matrites near man by man, and Saul the son of Kish was taken by lot..... **12.1** Samuel said to all Israel, "I have listened to you in all that you have said to me, and have set a king over you. **12.2** See, it is the king who leads you now; I am old and gray ...."

1 Samuel (Cont'd)

King Saul

14.52 There was hard fighting against the Philistines all the days of Saul; and when Saul saw any strong or valiant warrior, he took him into his service. **16.15** And Saul's servants said to him, "…. **16.16** Let our lord now command the servants who attend you to look for someone who is skillful in playing the lyre; … he will play it, and you will feel better." **16.17** So Saul said to his servants, "Provide for me someone who can play well, and bring him to me." **16.21** And David came to Saul, and entered his service. Saul loved him greatly, and he became his armor-bearer. **17.1** Now the Philistines gathered their armies for battle.

David & Goliath

17.4 And there came out from the camp of the Philistines a champion named Goliath, of Gath, whose height was six cubits and a span. **17.8** He stood and shouted to the ranks of Israel, "Why have you come out to draw up for battle? Am I not a Philistine, and are you not servants of Saul? Choose a man for yourselves, and let him come down to me. **17.9** If he is able to fight with me and kill me, then we will be your servants; but if I prevail against him and kill him, then you shall be our servants and serve us." **17.11** When Saul and all Israel heard these words of the Philistine, they were dismayed and greatly afraid.

17.32 David said to Saul, "Let no one's heart fail because of him; your servant will go and fight with this Philistine." **17.48** When the Philistine drew nearer to meet David, David ran quickly toward the battle line to meet the Philistine. **17.49** David put his hand in his bag, took out a stone, slung it, and struck the Philistine on his forehead; the stone sank into his forehead, and he fell face down on

1 Samuel (Cont'd)

the ground. **17.50** So David prevailed over the Philistine with a sling and a stone, striking down the Philistine and killing him; there was no sword in David's hand. **17.51** .... When the Philistines saw that their champion was dead, they fled.

Saul & David

18.7 And the women sang to one another as they made merry, "Saul has killed his thousands, and David his ten thousands." **18.8** Saul was very angry, for this saying displeased him. He said, "They have ascribed to David ten thousands, and to me they ascribed thousands; what more can he have but the kingdom?" **18.9** So Saul eyed David from that day on.

19.1 Saul spoke with his son Jonathan and with all his servants about killing David. But Saul's son Jonathan took great delight in David. **19.2** Jonathan told David, "My father Saul is trying to kill you ...." **19.18** Now David fled and escaped ....

25.1 Now Samuel died; and all Israel assembled and mourned for him .... **31.1** Now the Philistines fought against Israel; and the men of Israel fled before the Philistines, and many fell on Mount Gilboa. **31.8** The next day, when the Philistines came to strip the dead, they found Saul and his three sons fallen on Mount Gilboa.

Extracted From the Book of 2 Samuel

King David

1.11 Then David took hold of his clothes and tore them; and all the men who were with him did the same. **1.12** They mourned and wept, and fasted until evening for Saul and for his son Jonathan, and for the army ..., and for the house of Israel because they had fallen by the sword. **2.3** David brought up the men who were with him, every one with his household; and they settled in the towns of Hebron. **2.4** Then the people of Judah came, and there they anointed David king over the house of Judah.

3.2 Sons were born to David at Hebron: his firstborn was Amnon, of Ahinoam of Jezreel; **3.3** his second, Chileab of Abigail ...; the third, Absalom son of Maacah, daughter of King Talmai of Geshur; **3.4** the fourth, Adonijah son of Haggith; the fifth, Shephatiah son of Abital; **3.5** and the sixth, Ithream, of David's wife Eglah ....

5.1 Then all the tribes of Israel came to David at Hebron, and said, ".... **5.2** For some time, while Saul was king over us, it was you who led out Israel and brought it in ...." **5.3** So all the elders ... anointed David king over Israel.

5.6 The king and his men marched to Jerusalem against the Jebusites, the inhabitants of the land .... **5.7** ... David took the stronghold .... **5.9** and named it the city of David. **5.13** In Jerusalem, after he came from Hebron, David took more concubines and wives; and more sons and daughters were born to David. **5.14** These are the names of those who were born to him in Jerusalem: Shammua, Shobab, Nathan, Solomon, **5.15** Ibhar, Elishua, Nepheg, Japhia, **5.16** Elishama, Eliada, and Eliphelet.

8.1 Some time afterward, David attacked the Philistines and subdued them .... **8.2** He also defeated the Moabites .... **8.3** David also struck down King Hadadezer ... as he went to restore his monument at the river Euphrates. **8.5** When the Arameans of

2 Samuel (Cont'd)

Damascus came to help King Hadadezer ... David killed ... the Arameans. **8.6** Then David put garrisons among the Arameans of Damascus; and the Arameans became servants to David and brought tribute. **8.14** He put garrisons in Edom ....

David & Bathsheba

11.1 In the spring of the year, the time when kings go out to battle, David sent Joab with his officers and all Israel with him; they ravaged the Ammonites, and besieged Rabbah. But David remained at Jerusalem.

11.2 It happened, late one afternoon, when David rose from his couch and was walking about on the roof of the king's house, that he saw from the roof a woman bathing; the woman was very beautiful. **11.3** David sent someone to inquire about the woman. It was reported, "This is Bathsheba ..., the wife of Uriah the Hittite. **11.4** So David sent messengers to get her, and she came to him, and he lay with her .... Then she returned to her house. **11.5** The woman conceived, and she sent and told David, "I am pregnant."

11.6 So David sent word to Joab, "Send me Uriah the Hittite." And Joab sent Uriah to David. **11.7** When Uriah came to him, David asked how Joab and the people fared, and how the war was going. **11.8** Then David said to Uriah, "Go down to your house, and wash your feet." Uriah went out of the king's house, and there followed him a present from the king. **11.9** But Uriah slept at the entrance of the king's house with all the servants of his lord, and did not go down to his house. **11.10** When they told David, "Uriah did not go down to his house," David said to Uriah, "You have just come from a journey. Why did you not go down to house?" **11.11** Uriah said to David, "... Israel and Judah remain in booths; and my lord Joab and the servants of my lord are camping in the open field; shall I then go to my house, to eat and to drink, and to lie with my wife? As you live, ... I will not do such a thing." **11.12** Then David said to Uriah, "Remain here today also, and tomorrow I will send you back." ....

11.14 In the morning David wrote a letter to Joab, and sent it by the hand of Uriah. **11.15** In the letter he wrote, "Set Uriah in the forefront of the hardest fighting, and then draw back from him, so that he may be struck down and die." **11.16** As Joab was besieging the city, he assigned Uriah to the place where he knew there were valiant warriors. **11.17** The men of the city came out and fought with Joab; and some of the servants of David among the people fell. Uriah ... was killed as well.

11.26 When the wife of Uriah heard that her husband was dead, she made lamentations for him. **11.27** When the mourning was over, David sent and brought her to his house, and she became his wife, and bore him a son .... 12.24 ..., and he named him Solomon.

Rape of Tamar

13.1 Some time passed. David's son Absalom had a beautiful sister whose name was Tamar; and David's son Amnon fell in love with her. **13.2** Amnon was so tormented that he made himself ill because of his sister Tamar, for she was a virgin and it seemed impossible to Amnon to do anything to her.

13.3 But Amnon had a friend whose name was Jonadab, the son of David's brother Shimeah; and Jonadab was a very crafty man. **13.4** He said to him, "O son of the king, why are you so haggard morning after morning? Will you not tell me?" Amnon said to him, "I love Tamar, my brother Absalom's sister." **13.5** Jonadab said to him, "Lie down on your bed, and pretend to be ill; and when your father comes to see you, say to him, 'Let my sister Tamar come and give me something to eat, and prepare the food in my sight, so that I may see it and eat it from her hand.'"

13.6 So Amnon lay down, and pretended to be ill; and when the king came to see him, Amnon said to the king, "Please let my sister Tamar come and make a couple of cakes in my sight, so that I may eat from her hand." **13.7** Then David sent home to Tamar, saying, "Go to your brother Amnon's house, and prepare food for him."

13.8 So Tamar went to her brother Amnon's house, where he was lying down. She took dough, kneaded it, made cakes in his sight, and baked the cakes. **13.9** Then she took the pan and set them out before him, but he refused to eat. Amnon said, "Send out everyone from me." So everyone went out from him. **13.10** Then Amnon said to Tamar, "Bring the food into the chamber, so that I may eat from your hand." So Tamar took the cakes she had made, and brought them into the chamber to Amnon her brother. **13.11** But when she brought them near him to eat, he took hold of her and said to her, "Come, lie with me, my sister." **13.12** She answered him, "No, my brother, do not force me: for such a thing is not done in Israel; do not do anything so vile! **13.13** As for me, where could I carry my shame? And as for you, you would be as one of the scoundrels in Israel. Now, therefore, I beg you, speak to the king; for he will not withhold me from you." **13.14** But he would not listen to her; and being stronger than she, he forced her and lay with her. **13.15** Then …. **13.19** … Tamar … went away, crying aloud as she went.

13.20 Her brother Absalom said to her, "Has Amnon your brother been with you? Be quiet for now, my sister; he is your brother; do not take this to heart." So Tamar remained, a desolate woman, in her brother Absalom's house.

13.21 When King David heard of all these things, he became very angry, but he would not punish his son Amnon, because he loved him, for he was his firstborn. **13.22** But Absalom spoke to Amnon neither good nor bad; for Absalom hated Amnon, because he had raped his sister Tamar.

Absalom

13.23 After two full years Absalom had sheepshearers ... and Absalom invited all of the king's sons. **13.28** Then Absalom commanded his servants, "Watch when Amnon's heart is merry with wine, and when I say to you, 'Strike Amnon,' then kill him ....'" **13.29** So the servants of Absalom did to Amnon as Absalom had commanded. Then all the king's sons rose, and each mounted his mule and fled. **13.36** As ... the king's sons arrived, and raised their voices and wept; ... the king and all his servants also wept very bitterly. **13.37** .... David mourned for his son day after day.

13.38 Absalom, having fled to Geshur, stayed there three years. **13.39** And the heart of the king went out, yearning for Absalom; for he was now consoled over the death of Amnon. **14.21** Then the king .... **14.23** ... brought Absalom to Jerusalem. **14.24** The king said, "Let him go to his own house; he is not to come into my presence." So Absalom went to his own house, and did not come into the king's presence.

14.25 Now in all Israel there was no one to be praised so much for his beauty as Absalom; from the sole of his foot to the crown of his head there was no blemish in him. **14.27** There were born to

2 Samuel (Cont'd)

Absalom three sons, and one daughter whose name was Tamar; she was a beautiful woman.

14.28 So Absalom lived two full years in Jerusalem, without coming into the king's presence. **14.29** Then Absalom sent …. **14.33** … to the king, and … he summoned Absalom. So he came to the king, and prostrated himself with his face to the ground before the king; and the king kissed Absalom.

15.1 After this Absalom got himself a chariot and horses, and fifty men to run ahead of him. **15.6** … Absalom stole the hearts of the people of Israel. **16.15** Now Absalom and … the Israelites came to Jerusalem …. **18.6** So the army went out into the field against Israel; and the battle was fought …. **18.7** The men of Israel were defeated ….

18.9 Absalom was riding on his mule, and the mule went under the thick branches of a great oak. His head caught fast in the oak, and he was left hanging between heaven and earth, while the mule that was under him went on. **18.15** And ten young men … surrounded Absalom and struck him, and killed him. **18.33** The king was deeply moved, … and wept; and … he said, "O my son Absalom, my son, my son Absalom! Would I had died instead of you, O Absalom, my son, my son!"

The verses that follow are the translations of the King James Version of the Bible, written in the English of 1611 CE. The use of italics, which served a purpose in archaic English, has been ignored here.

The archaic English might be compared to the modern English of your own Bible. That should show that the content is essentially the same whatever the translation.

Adonijah

1.1 Now king David was old and stricken in years; and they covered him with clothes, but he gat no heat. **1.2** Wherefore his servants said unto him, Let there be sought for my lord the king a young virgin: and let her stand before the king, and let her cherish him, and let her lie in thy bosom, that my lord the king may get heat. **1.3** So they sought for a fair damsel throughout all the coasts of Israel and found Abishag a Shunammite, and brought her to the king. **1.4** And the damsel was very fair; and cherished the king, and ministered to him: but the king knew her not.

1.5 Then Adonijah … exalted himself, saying, I will be king: and he prepared him chariots and horsemen, and fifty men to run before him. **1.6** And his father had not displeased him at any time in saying, Why hast thou done so? and he also was a very goodly man; and his mother bare him after Absalom.

1 Kings (Cont'd)

1.15 And Bathsheba went in unto the king …. **1.16** And Bathsheba bowed, and did obeisance unto the king. And the king said, What wouldest thou? **1.17** And she said unto him, My lord, thou swearest … unto thine handmaid, saying , Assuredly Solomon thy son shall reign after me, and he shall sit upon my throne. **1.18** And now, behold, Adonijah reigneth; and … thou knowest it not. **1.29** And the king sware, …. **1.30** … saying, Assuredly Solomon thy son shall reign after me, and he shall sit upon my throne in my stead; even so will I certainly do this day.

1.41 And Adonijah and all the guests that were with him heard it as they had made an end of eating …. **1.49** And all the guests that were with Adonijah were afraid, and rose up, and went every man his way. **1.50** And Adonijah feared because of Solomon, and arose, and went …. **1.51** And it was told Solomon, saying, Behold Adonijah feareth king Solomon …. **1.52** And Solomon said, If he will prove himself a worthy man, there shall not a hair of him fall to the earth: but if wickedness shall be found in him, he shall die. **1.53** So king Solomon sent, and … he came and bowed himself to king Solomon: and Salomon said unto him, Go to thine house.

King Solomon

2.1 Now the days of David drew nigh that he should die …. **2.10** So David slept with his fathers, and was buried in the city of David. **2.12** Then sat Solomon upon the throne of David his father; and his kingdom was established greatly.

2.13 And Adonijah … came to Bathsheba …. **2.17** And he said, Speak, I pray thee, unto Solomon the king, … that he give me Abishag … to wife. **2.18** And Bathsheba said, Well; I will speak for thee unto the king. **2.19** Bathsheba therefore went unto king

Solomon, to speak unto him for Adonijah .... **2.20** Then she said, I desire one small petition of thee; I pray thee, say me not nay. And the king said unto her, Ask on, my mother: for I will not say thee nay. **2.21** And she said, Let Abishag ... be given to Adonijah thy brother to wife.

2.22 And king Solomon answered and said unto his mother, And why dost thou ask Abishag ... for Adonijah? ask for him the kingdom also; for he is mine elder brother .... **2.24** ... Adonijah shall be put to death this day. **2.46** .... And the kingdom was established in the hand of Solomon.

References

SCRIPTURAL REFERENCES

KINGS JAMES BIBLE, 1611.

NIV STUDY BIBLE, New International Version, Zondervon, Grand Rapids, 2002.

THE FIVE BOOKS OF MOSES, A New Translation with Introductions, Commentary, and Notes by Everett Fox, Schocken Books, New York, 1995.

THE JEWISH STUDY BIBLE, Jewish Publication Society TANAKH Translation, Oxford University Press, New York, 2004.

THE MacARTHUR STUDY BIBLE, New King James Version, John MacArthur, Editor, Thomas Nelson, Nashville, Tennessee, 1997.

THE NEW OXFORD ANNOTATIED BIBLE, New Revised Standard Version, 3rd Edition, Oxford University Press, New York, 2001.

OTHER REFERENCES

Friedman, Richard Elliott, *"Who Wrote the Bible?"* Summit Books, New York, 1987, reprinted HarperSan-Francisco, 1997.

Lamp, Walter, *"Biblical Verses, A Frank Study of the Old Testament and Hebrew Bible,"* RunningLight Publishing, Reno, Nevada, 2012.

Lamp, Walter, *"THE TAMAR BIBLE, The First Judeo-Christian Scripture,"* RunningLight Publishing, Reno, Nevada, 2009.

Citation Index

OLD TESTAMENT/
HEBREW BIBLE

HISTORICAL BOOKS

Index

Sabbath, 27, 48, 91,
Sackcloth, 64,
Sacred, 6, 9, 35, 36,
Sacrifice, 6, 74, 91,
Samson, 14, 29, 48, 66, 82,
Samuel, Book of, 110,
Sarah, 11, 22, 33, 37, 38,
　65, 82, 104,
Sarai, 11. *See* Sarah.
Saul, 67. *See* King Saul.
Schocken Bible, 78,
Seduction, 22, 45, 46, 72,
　80,
Semen, 79, 80,
Serpent, 13, 25,
Seth, 88, 89,
Shelah, 35,
Sin, sinful, 15, 87, 89, 96-
　101, 103, 106, 107, 109,
　111-113,
Sistine Chapel, 69,
Slave(ry), 29, 30, 45, 57,
　66, 74, 91,
Sodom, 14, 15, 54-56, 78,
　79, **95-114**,
Sodomy, 79,
Solomon, 11-13, 36, 37, 66.
　Also see King Solomon.
Sorcerers, 34,
Soul, 62,
Southern Kingdom. *See*
　Kingdom of Judah.
Spurious, 92,

Subjugation, 17, 23, 24, ,

Tamar (daughter of King
　David), 6, 14, 39, 66,
　86, 101,
Tamar (daughter of
　Absalom), 66,
Tamar (wife of Er), 15, 35,
　36, 57, 66, 79, 85,
Tamar Bible, 6,
Tanakh, 65. *Same as*
　Hebrew Bible.
Taxation, 26,
Temple, 7, 33, 39, 56, 91,
Temple prostitutes, 56, 57,
　81,
Ten Commandments, 5, 10,
　26, 27, 30, 49, 71, 89,
　109,
Torah, 1, 78, 96. *Also* Five
　Books of Moses,
　Pentateuch.
Touch(ing), 25, 53, 102,
Trans-dressing, 79,
Transform(ation), 9, 113,
　114,
Transgendered, 54,
Translation(s), 2, 4, 5, 8, 60,
　78, 106,

www.ingramcontent.com/pod-product-compliance
Lightning Source LLC
Chambersburg PA
CBHW050122280326
41933CB00010B/1203